Y0-DBO-737

CLEARING THE TANGLED WOOD

POETRY AS A WAY OF SEEING THE WORLD

JAMES LAWLESS

ACADEMICA PRESS
BETHESDA – DUBLIN - PALO ALTO

Library of Congress Cataloging-in-Publication Data

Lawless, James.
 Clearing the tangled wood: poetry as a way of seeing the world / by James
Lawless.
     p. cm. – (Irish Research Series : #56)
 Includes bibliographical references and index.
 IRS - #54
 ISBN-13: 978-1-933146-60-7
 ISBN-10: 1-933146-60-5
 1. Poetics. 2. Poetry--History and criticism. I. Title.
 PN1136.L39 2009
 808.1--dc22
                              2009000663

Copyright 2009 by James Lawless

All rights reserved. Printed in the United States of America. No part of this book
may be used or reproduced in any manner whatsoever without written permission
except in the case of brief quotations embodied in critical articles and reviews.

Academica Press, LLC
Box 60728
Cambridge Station
Palo Alto, CA. 94306

Website: www.academicapress.com

to order: 650-329-0685

PN
1136
L39
2009

CONTENTS

FOREWORD

Poetry is not so much an escape from reality as an intense confrontation with it. The words of an artist convey a heightened sense of life, even as they realise the genius of a given language. A poet may begin as a dreamer, but the moment of art is that in which the pressure of the actual is contained by an unexpected but appropriate form.

In this luminous and wide-ranging meditation, James Lawless considers the dynamics of creation. For him the poet is one who, in reconnecting us with our buried selves, also invents a new way of seeing the world.

If the energy of life is a desire for form, then the artist seeks a language in which to capture all that newness. Necessarily, those who try to define something as yet unknown must work in a known idiom, but their originality allows them to put that idiom to strange, unprecedented uses. This often calls for a transcendence of inherited bipolar notions of the world, of sexuality, of class and even of the self.

James Lawless writes with the authority of one who knows that an artist doesn't just report ideas or feelings: he or she can also invent them or at least offer a new naming. Again and again, whether he writes of Russian, Spanish, Irish or American artists, he reminds us that the poet is the kind of person who can survive confusion and report it with clarity.

James Lawless knows that poetry gets to those parts of the psyche which a more rational analysis cannot reach: and that such an expedition is necessary if our world is to be remade.

Declan Kiberd

PREFACE

Man is often more irrational than rational. Literal language fails to recognise this fully. Poetry, however, because of its different grammar and anarchic qualities, is capable of addressing this aspect of our lives. By offering an alternative way of seeing the world, it affords deeper insights into reality, and it helps us to see "as other". To enter the world of poetry, one must heighten one's state of consciousness, and surrender to its methods of observation. Suggestions on how to achieve this state are given in this work, and the process of creativity itself is discussed. Influences of other disciplines and texts are demarcated, and the evolution of poetry from oral to written to visual form is delineated. Examples are given of how poetry illuminates our ordinary, ideological and technological worlds. Some attention is also given to an examination of the role of the poet in society. Extracts from the works of various contemporary poets are cited, including a chapter on modern Irish poetry. However, in order to illustrate more fully the semantic, psychological and aesthetic enrichment which can be derived from poetry, and in an attempt to steer away – even if temporarily – from the hegemony of English, the poetry of three non-English poets (Salinas, Lorca and Pasternak) is appraised in some detail. This work concludes with a vindication of the value of poetry in the twenty first century, not only as an art form in itself, but also as an essential, interpretative tool in a fragmented world.

ACKNOWLEDGEMENTS

I wish to gratefully acknowledge the poets and writers living and dead whom I cite or quote from in this work. All of them hopefully are sourced in the notes, bibliography and index. A special word of thanks for their support and encouragement to my wife Margaret and our family and to Brendan Ryan, Declan Kiberd, Brendan Kennelly, John Montague, Nuala Ní Dhomhnaill, Michael D Higgins, Katie Donovan, Pat Boran, Gerald Dawe, Joe Woods and the staffs of Poetry Ireland and of the Instituto Cervantes, Dublin; and in the USA my gratitude to Thomas Kinsella, Eamon Grennan, George O'Brien, Robert Redfern-West, Tiffany Randall and Ginger McNally.

1 INTRODUCTION

His gaze those bars keep passing is so misted
with tiredness, it can take in nothing more.
He feels as though a thousand bars existed,
and no more world beyond them than before.

This stanza from Rilke's *Panther* (1904) presents an animal of enormous energy restricted and stupefied by cage bars. Sometimes an image will appear, only to be killed by his trapped and frustrated heart. The poem is a good metaphor for the conflict between the inner vision of the poet and the destructive external world.

Poetry is not merely writing, as some would have us believe,[1] but in many cases it is the only means which the "speaking animal" has "to shift the limits of its enclosure" (Kristeva, 1980:33).

Freud credits poetry with the power of liberating the unconscious (Cheselka, 1987:70). His role was to turn the study of the unconscious into a science, and he very effectively showed man as a frequently more irrational than rational being. There are limitations on literal language to express our inner selves. Our thoughts go round in circles, but our language is linear, as Bergson (1910) points out. If we take Nabokov's definition of poetry as "the mysteries of the irrational perceived through rational words" (Winokur, 1989:78), we see the importance of poetry as a key to unravelling some of the complexities of our innermost psyches.

The more we accustom ourselves to seeing, or perhaps to half-seeing things in a certain way, the more reluctant we are to see "otherness". Watzlawick et al (1974) have illustrated how difficult it is for people to effect change in society, when they are blinkered by having to work within already constricted, conceptual frameworks. And Whiting (Rogers, 1982:113) points out: "people have a set of latent alternative behaviour that can be activated by changed conditions."

I propose that poetry offers an alternative way of seeing the world (particularly in the context of increasing standardisation imposed on us by multi-media and information technology). It uses a different grammar to present insights and meanings, normally lost in literal language. It has the effect of jolting our system out of predictable expectations of meaning, and of activating our vision into areas formerly left dormant.[2] If we could develop the sense of seeing "as other", imagine the wonderful repercussions that could have for mutual understanding in the world.

To enter the world of poetry, one must suspend belief (or disbelief, as some would argue) of a concrete existence and trust its method of observation, with the goal of semantic and spiritual enrichment.

This work proposes to examine some of the ways in which poetry pictures the world, and the meanings it finds, or attempts to find. To endeavour to achieve this end, certain conditions, which I propose to discuss in the following pages, are necessary

a heightened state of consciousness;

some knowledge of what is involved in creating a poem, and the reader's role in this;

an understanding of the semiotic content of poetry;

a realisation that a poem is part of a network of other texts and other worlds;

an appreciation of the interconnectedness or conflict from other disciplines, particularly philosophy and science;

an insight into poetic methods from oral to visual, and combinations thereof;

a mindfulness of the poet's role in society, as illuminator of quotidian, ideological and technological worlds.

I wish to glance briefly at modern Irish poetry and show it as a fusion of binary vision in male and female with a dual heritage of Irish and English languages enriching each other.

I wish to demonstrate also, how in an agnostic age, the spiritual demands on poetry are even greater, and how it has taken on the role of interpretative tool to discover meaning and the self. In so doing, I hope to refute the criticisms of those, who, from Plato onwards, have denigrated poetry for being illusory, and poets for being unstable or even effeminate.

And in the light of increasing contamination of the world by man, I hope to show that poetry matters, that it is no featherweight,[3] and that it can help us to see ourselves in a more ecologically-conscious way as "guests" (as Pasternak says), rather than as owners or conquerors of existence.

While I shall refer to various poets throughout the course of the work, I intend to conclude by singling out three non-English poets in particular: Salinas, Lorca and Pasternak. I choose these poets for their intrinsic value, and as illustrative of three distinct approaches to poetry, which hopefully, this work will touch upon. But I also choose them for the purpose of thus being afforded the opportunity of voyaging beyond our own hegemonic, linguistic ken, in an attempt "to see as other".

I single out Pedro Salinas, because his search for meaning is so sharp, so pared down, always in flux as he takes us through the looking glass of reality, enabling us to see with new eyes.

Federico García Lorca is included because of the dual encoding in his poetry, the deep metaphors of the grammar of poetry itself, and the deeper oneiric symbolism to conceal his sexual orientation.

Finally, Boris Pasternak appears, as the pure poet, the living poem; even his prose works involved reflections on poetry. He could not escape living his life as a tragic work of art. His poetry is rich in symbolism and vision.

These, and other poets, I hope will illustrate the riches: semantic, psychological and aesthetic, which can be derived from poetry.

Because of the multi-faceted nature of poetry, and because it covers such a wide berth, I shall confine my arguments mainly — except for other references *en passant* — to poets of the twentieth and twenty first century.

Translations from Spanish and Irish in this work, unless where otherwise stated, are my own.

NOTES

[1] J.M.G. Le Clezio downgrades the written arts by equating all forms of writing

> Poetry, novels, short stories are remarkable antiquities which no longer fool anyone. Poems, narratives – what's the use of them? There is nothing but writing left (Barthes, 1987:64).

[2] P. Bürger (1992:20), echoing Walter Benjamin (q.v.), points out that

> the task of all new art is to disturb automatised modes of perception through the very organisation of the artistic material, and thus force the recipient of the work to adopt a new way of seeing.

[3] Don Marquis likened the publishing of a volume of verse to the "dropping of a rose-petal down the Grand Canyon and waiting for an echo" (Winokur:168).

2 A HEIGHTENED STATE OF CONSCIOUSNESS

Our thoughts are often clouded and gnarled by our environment; our concentration and feelings can be affected by whether we are at ease or not, or by the attitude of peers etc. So how does one "clear" the mind, as it were, for the purpose of poetic receptivity?

Meditative preparedness, which Wordsworth talks about in his preface to *Lyrical Ballads* (1798) as a way of gaining poetic knowledge, could also be latched onto by the reader as a way of being in a state of readiness for reception of a text. Barthes (1967) talks of the consumer of poetry encountering the word frontally i.e., no longer guided in advance with rational intention. It achieves a condition where, like in a dictionary, it can live without its article i.e., it is reduced to a sort of zero state. The word is a category, it initiates discourse. The poem is "full of gaps, of discontinuous speech, full of lights, filled with absences" (p.38).

According to Indian thought, knowledge is different when one is in different states of consciousness. It cannot be removed from the situation of the knower. Rilke represents consciousness as a pyramid, with everyday literal perceptions at the apex, and the transcendental at the base (Yarrow, 1985:2). A heightened state of consciousness enables us to create form, patterns and meaning, just as they appear on the point of happening. It is a condition where action is held in poise, like the balance of a trapeze artist. It leaves one open to total receptivity. It is what James Joyce meant, when he spoke of "epiphanies".

How does one achieve this state? Yarrow suggests a method which involves a progressive reduction of effort, until one is simply conscious of being conscious, alert without engaging in activity. He mentions Transcendental Meditation as one way of achieving this wholeness.[1] However, he is quick to point out that the restful condition achieved is not "quiescent... but rather a vital part of tuning up the mechanism by which we interact with the world" (p.4).

He discloses how the writer sometimes cuts the reader off from his normal assumptions of the world by shock devices.[2] The reader of course must negate *a priori* beliefs and create a willingness to think otherwise. Thus, as Yarrow points out, a transformation takes place, where one global-view is displaced by another, and the reader is ready to make sense of the world anew. "It is the experience of the potential of consciousness which can then project itself onto the organisation of physical and verbal relationships" (p.7). This attempt, to use rationality to go beyond the limitations of language, has echoes in it of surrealists or even of mystics

> The goal is to discover a more extensive kind of being-in-language, and the conjunction of self, language and world both as process-in-formation and as a nodal point of that ongoing creative process is what links the preoccupation of writers with that of philosophers and mystics (p.8).

However, the mystical analogy, if constricted in a Christian sense, could be interpreted by a non-religious person as "passing the buck" of the unknowable, and that which cannot be expressed, to God (cf. San Juan de la Cruz).[3] Nevertheless, his reference to Transcendental Meditation as a means of achieving a heightened state of consciousness appears to have some validity: while in this state – one which, as he points out (p.16), is common to many artists – EEG readings indicate that brain-wave functioning is at its most coherent. Thus, in order to achieve a *gestalt*, we are confronted with the paradox of withdrawing consciousness from an object so as to be more aware of its potentiality, "and in the process to sharpen and hone its focus" (p.9) (cf. Keats' *Negative Capability*, or Hopkins' *Inscape*). It must not be forgotten that understanding is an organic process, and that the physical and unvoiced mantra effect of TM is not unlike the rhythmic ritual of early poetic recitation, giving insights to a "communal or archetypal nature, as also to a perception of linguistic resonances much fuller than surface levels of meaning" (p.10). It is worth considering in this context, the Vedic view of pure language, as an accurately encoded system of vibratory equivalents, which physically realise the world.

Nevertheless, if such methods fail, and one does not succeed in achieving such a transcendental state, all hope is not lost. One could lie in a darkened cell with a stone on one's belly, as was the preparatory custom of ancient Irish *filidhe* prior to composition. Or failing that, one could take Stephen Spender's (1962) advice in *The Making of a Poem*, where he cites Schiller's practical technique of placing rotten apples under the lid of his desk (Vernon, 1970:62). This had the effect of banishing all other distractions, and enabled him to channel his concentration totally into the one area of poetic composition.

NOTES

[1] Yarrow further maintains that TM works, not only because it "tunes up" the mechanism, but also, because it "solves" the problem of language itself, "by passing the referential level altogether" (p.15). Such a state is not dissimilar to the Zen Buddhist non-judgmental awakening, as an aid to a non-biased view of the world, a process, which, as Marilyn French points out (1985:135), never allows "the 'I' to fare without the 'non-I.'" Octavio Paz (1970) cites Buddha

> Only the man free of his necessity and the tyranny of authority will be able to contemplate fully his own nothingness.

[2] The subversive power of poetry could be considered in the context of Walt Whitman's use of religious language and poetic structure in *Song of Myself* (1855) to undermine prevailing dogma: "The scent of these armpits is aroma finer than prayers." He mocks the sacred scent of incense, preferring the natural smell of human perspiration. A similar opposition to institutions is also evident in the Irish Fenian cycle of poems, where Ossian converses with St. Patrick. Ossian, like Whitman, prefers the golden rays of the sun as opposed to the metal shine of a chalice, and he berates Patrick for his subservience to the bell, summoning one to a cloistered world. Austin Clarke recaptures the mood and early Irish metres of the original poem (*Agallamh na Seanórach {The Colloquy of the Old Men}*) in his rendition: *The Blackbird of Derrycairn* (Mahon, 1972:65)

> Stop, stop and listen for the bough top
> Is whistling and the sun is brighter
> Than God's own shadow in the cup now!
> Forget the hour-bell. Mournful matins
> Will sound as well, Patric, at nightfall.

[3] A distinction must be made between mystical (in a Christian sense) and visionary. The latter, as Levi (1990) points out, is more personal and more rooted in earthy experience. While not denying the allegorical beauty of the poetry of San Juan de la Cruz, his drawing of the way to the soul's union with God appears today in the words of Levi (p.88) "like one of those Victorian games of snakes and ladders constructed for children by Bible societies". Dante is visionary, but as Levi shows, his Hell is theatrical, a literary device, not meant to be taken literally. Blake is visionary, despite his "heretical" reference to a "hook-nosed Christ," in his poem, *Jerusalem*. Eliot's *The Waste Land* is visionary, although it is interpreted by some as pessimistic. The iconoclastic Kavanagh is visionary, particularly in his early Monaghan poems, where his vision of poetry is trapped by the "peasant's prayer", just as the apparently hedonistic Larkin is visionary when he is at his loneliest as in *High Windows*.

3 WITNESSING BIRTHS

I imagine this midnight moment's forest:
Something else is alive
Beside the clock's loneliness
And this blank page where my fingers move.

In the poem, *The Thought Fox* (1957), by Ted Hughes, the poet is confronted by the blank page. He must wait patiently for creativity to take hold, for a new word to appear through the loneliness. The clock ticks on, and slowly, the fox (creativity) emerges, "delicately as the dark snow", – initially only the trace: nose, two hesitant eyes "that now/And again now, and now, and now/Sets neat prints into the snow". But then, more and more of him appears autonomously ("coming about his own business"), until one can smell his "sharp hot stink" entering the dark hole of the poet's head: "The clock ticks,/The page is printed."

Hughes himself has this to say about the creation of this poem, which of course is about creativity itself

> If I had not caught the real fox there in the words I would never have saved the poem. I would have thrown it into the wastepaper basket as I have thrown so many other hunts that did not get what I was after. As it is, every time I read the poem the fox comes up again out of the darkness and steps into my head. And I suppose that long after I am gone, as long as a copy of the poem exists, every time anyone reads it, the fox will get up

somewhere out in the darkness and come walking towards them... and I made it.

The idea of poetry springing into conception and following its own laws (usually, as mentioned earlier, after an incubation period involving mental relaxation),[1] is captured in the tiger image in Milosz's *Ars Poetica* (1988)

> a thing is brought forth which we didn't know we
> had in us,
> so we blink our eyes, as if a tiger had sprung out
> and stood in the light, lashing his tail.

The tiger image is also used by the Mexican Ruvalcaba (1988:64) in his minimalist poem, *Apuntes (Notes)*: *"La mano escribiendo poesia: el tigre huyendo de la jaula"* ("The hand that writes poetry is the tiger fleeing his cage"). This also brings to mind Rilke's caged panther, and raises the subject of intertextuality, which we will address later.

The parallel of creating a poem and giving birth is expressed by Jimmy Santiago Baco, a Chicano, wounded into poetry by prison life

> Every poem is an infant labored into birth, and I am drenched with
> sweating effort (tired from the pain and hurt of being a man, in the poem I
> transform myself into woman, and thus transcend the pain and give birth to
> words) (Rich, 1993:208-9).

Charles Tomlinson (1986) describes the birth within a poem itself: "We bring/To a kind of birth all we can name/And named, it echoes in our being" ("Adam," from *The Way of the World*).

Emily Dickinson (Sewall, 1963:53) puts the matter more gently, when, in her quest for the right word, there came unexpectedly

That portion of the vision
The word applied to fill.
Not unto nomination
The cherubim reveal.
(*Bolts of Melody*)

The fox or tiger, for her, becomes an angel, who arrives with a vision to supply the missing word, and all her hesitation ceases. Inspiration comes irrationally, yet, for all poets, a meditative preparedness is necessary (see Note[1]). All doors must be open, so that "invisible guests", as Milosz says, can "come in and out at will". This heightened awareness of creativity can of course be equally applied to the reader,[2] whose role is also creative in ensuring complete receptivity of the text. The ego must be abandoned as individuality is pushed towards a universality of awareness.   The mind cleared, is alert and waiting. Kafka's self-preparation (1954:54) is worth recording

> There's no need to leave your house. Stay at your desk and listen. Don't even listen, just wait. Don't even wait, be perfectly still and alone. The world will unmask itself to you, it can't do otherwise, it will writhe before you in raptures.[3]

Louis MacNeice reinforces the idea of words choosing the poet rather than the reverse: "I watched the words come and drink at my mind" (Stanford, 1980:98). Housman (p.160) describes the process as a "secretion," while Eliot, more crudely, says it is similar to "defecation" (Winokur, 1987:107). Robert Graves explains, how at the beginning of a poem, the poet's mind is in a "trance-like suspension of his normal habits of thought" (see Note[2]). Most importantly of all, however, is the realisation that a poem is never, as Robert Frost puts it, "a thought to begin with" (Stanford:160). It is more like a "tantalising vagueness," which in its aleatory nature, finds its thought and succeeds, or doesn't find it, and comes to nothing, like the hit-or-miss chances of spermfish floating about, in their quest for birth.

The struggle for conception is also the dominant feature in Marge Piercy's muse, which like Hughes', also comes at night, walking back and forth across the belly

> in boots with cleats cursing and kicking and singing the praises of the unborn poems and the untold stories till they swarm like fish babies ripping the flanks of sheep (Mole, 1989:185).

Boldness is also needed: "Boldness in face of the blank sheet" was hailed by Pasternak as an attribute of talent (Heaney, 1988:164). As Ruvalcaba (p.64) puts it: "todo papel en blanco/contiene/un poema ensimismado" ("Every blank paper/ contains/a poem lost in thought"). Or perhaps, if put more colloquially, one could say: one needs the courage to "bungee-jump" with pen and paper.

NOTES

[1] Liam Hudson points out that our brains are at their most efficient when allowed to switch from phases of intense concentration to ones in which we exert no conscious control at all (Gregory: 171). He cites, as an example, the remarkable case of Rainer Maria Rilke, who endured a decade of depression (1912-22), during which he was unable to write. "Utterance and release eventually came in the form of continuous writing for eighteen days, producing over 1,200 lines of some of the most beautiful poetry ever written (*Sonnets to Orpheus*, and the *Duino Elegies*), and done largely without correction, as if he were taking dictation. Einstein recognised such a state when he declared that creative scientists are the ones with access to their dreams. The implication of this statement, according to Hudson, is that

> in order to innovate, the scientist, like anyone else, must break the grip on his imagination that our powers of logical-seeming story-telling impose. We must be willing to subvert the conventional wisdom on which our everyday competence depends (p.172).

Instead of concentrating on what he calls the seemingly "largely barren exercise" of IQ tests, he recommends a renewal of interest in the work of Francis Galton, who tried to identify "the extent to which each individual can retrieve apparently irrational ideas, sift them, and put them to some constructive use" (p.172). The poet Richard Eberhart describes creativity similarly, borrowing from physics, to give force to his images

> In the rigours of composition... the poet's mind is a filament, informed with irrational vitality of energy as it was discovered in our time in quantum mechanics. The quanta may shoot off in any way (Waterstone, 1988:1278).

Thus science and poetry can join forces, as twin hemispheres in a common pursuit, acting as creative energisers on a tired world.

[2] There are great readers just as there are great writers. As Derek Walcott (1986:324) points out, one could

> abandon writing for the slow-burning signals of the great, to be, instead their ideal reader, ruminative, voracious, making the love of masterpieces superior to attempting to repeat or outdo them and be the greatest reader in the world (*Volcano*).

Cf. Canetti's *Auto da Fe* (1935), where the character, Peter Kien structures his entire life around his chief pursuit: reading.

[3] For fear that Kafka is giving the impression here that the creative process is unproblematic, one has only to turn to Tchaikovsky, who in one of his letters (in which he discusses his method of composing) exclaims: "Sometimes one must do oneself violence, must sternly and pitilessly take part against oneself, before one can mercilessly erase things out with love and enthusiasm." *Kamenka, 25 June 1878* (Vernon: 59).

4 SEEING HIDDEN THINGS

4.1 The Spotted Chameleon

Before the advent of Sigmund Freud, unreason had been depicted as a "blind brute, enraged and stupid" (Bruner, 1986:140). Freud (1908) argued, however, that what we often perceived as nonsense was in fact a repository of the human condition and human intentions. Bruner (p.110), lends support to this insight by summarising John Austin's (1962) conclusions, noting that the greater part of human discourse is not factual or analytic, but has to do with requests, promises, affiliations, encouragements, threats and the like. As he puts it, we even create "bricks and mortar realities" like jails, to deal with people who fail to conform to "the felicity conditions on certain forms of promising".

Martin Croghan (1990:27) also accuses those who dismiss the phatic function of language of "intellectual elitism and an inability to cope with real language semantics as both closed and open systems".

Such apparently non-rational and underrated areas of speech are rich granaries of insight into the human condition, something which poetry, at least, does not fail to recognise.

Outsiderhood is an example of a condition, which most people try to hide or deny at all costs. They expend great energy, verbal, sartorial, behavioural – often dissimulating in the process – in order to act like chameleons, so that they can fit (invisibly) into whatever is the dominant landscape. Art has a place for an outsider, but not for a pretender, because as Adrienne Rich (1986:128) points out, the social person who is the poet may also try "to pass", but the price of external assimilation is internal division, where one is left

> to dream of the impossible safe place,
> the upside-down park and fountain
> sleeping on the ceiling
> that world inverted
> where left is always right
> where the shadows are really the body
> where we stay awake all night.

4.2 The Charging Horse

Harold Bloom (1976), applying the Oedipus complex theory to poetry, maintains that the young, aspiring poet must slay his poetic father to avoid paternal castration in his rivalry for the love of the mother, and in order to impose his own creativity.[1] Each poem – created out of a struggle between Eros and Thanatos – is, according to Bloom, a palimpsest, replacing or subverting what went before, but still carrying some of the older work with it. It expresses, in accordance with Lacanian theory, the young poet's longing to return to the safety of the mother's womb. He is prepared to sublimate for this homecoming, this higher goal, and in an attempt to fill the absence of his mother's body, he has recourse to art, where he can be stitched back inside a safe haven once more (cf. filmic *suture* or Aristotelian *catharsis*). This is also in keeping with Holland's theory (1968), which argues that a child's premature separation from the mother could explain an "absorption" in literature in later life (Princeton, 1993:999). The creative writer, according to Freud (p.136), possesses

> the puzzling ability of moulding a specific material into a faithful image of the creatures of his imagination, and then he is able to attach to this representation of his unconscious fantasies so much pleasurable gratification that, for a time at least, it is able to outweigh and release the suppressions.

Freud asserts that a pleasure once acquired cannot be given up, but merely transferred to something else (p.128). The uninhibited play of the child is transferred into the inhibited fantasies of adulthood, which are frequently, and sometimes unwittingly repressed wish-fulfilments. Deep down we are all Walter Mittys, the difference being however, that the creative writer makes use of his wishes as material for art. This in turn entices an audience who, for their part, take the work of art as stimulus and elaborate on it with their own unconscious desires (Princeton:998). However, it doesn't have to follow, as a corollary, that an artist is more neurotic than other people – something which Freud and his followers believed. Perhaps it is more accurate to say that the artist is one who *articulates* neurosis more than other people (cf. Eagleton, 1983:180).

Because of the freedom it affords in the association of ideas, the unconscious should, according to Freud, be nurtured, but in a controlled way, as a source of inspiration: "The ego must learn to control the charging horse that is the ID, but he needs to be a good rider" (Bruner:140). Notice how Freud has recourse to poetic language (metaphors) here in order to express his theory, and as regards the unconscious itself, he believed that metaphor (q.v.) and poetry are effective as decoding devices, particularly in interpreting dreams. Also the anarchic nature of the unconscious, when combined with the symbolist and metaphorical nature of poetry, could be very effective in expressing certain taboo subjects (cf. Lorca's oneiric symbolism, q.v.). And the so-called Freudian slip of the tongue is the ID of the unconscious trying to break through the rules and conventions of tolerated social behaviour: "the artificer" (unreason), as Bruner puts it (p.140), "driving a hard bargain in a transaction with the ego".

Our rational age fears the uncomfortable effect such an "artificer" can have. It creates euphemisms to avoid confronting unpleasant issues: "gone to his last rest," "his number two," "in the family way" etc.[2]

Apart from the more obvious ideological suppression of poetry in some countries which are politically unstable and which we shall look at later, there is another type of poetic censorship (q.v.) inside the great democracies themselves. It is involved more as an ethos rather than in the direct banning of individual books. It is like apartheid in that, according to Rich (1993:19), it "bans the social recognition and integration of poetry, and the imaginative powers it releases". Even Auden said: "to stink of poetry is unbecoming" (*Stir among the Dead* {Paulin, 1990:358}). People are forbidden to quote it, to pepper their speech with it, it is cissyish.[3] It is, as Rich says, "under house arrest" and "irrelevant to mass entertainment".

Nevertheless, despite the pressure, art will not bow down under social manipulation. As Becker (1994:xiii) points out, it aggressively refuses "to sustain society's illusions", and as we shall see, neither will it tolerate taboos within its parameters.

NOTES

[1] I cite here, as an example, the tugging and pulling-away relationship of the Spanish poets Francisco Brines and Claudio Rodríguez with their precursor father poet, Juan Ramón Jiménez, or consider in an Irish context, how many young poets and writers try to kill the shadows of Yeats and Joyce and emerge in their own light (cf. Ch. 7.1).

[2] Another attempt at semi-disguising (although perhaps considered somewhat Victorian nowadays) was to use the French term *enceinte* in polite English society. The Spanish term *embarazada*, in its secondary meaning, seems to look upon pregnancy as an embarrassment. (Is it perversely to do with viewing the shape, induced by the condition, as a type of deformation?). Despite my criticisms here, I am not advocating the use of their antithesis in such slang English terms as "up the pole," which is really another form of periphrasis – crude and sexist this time – which fails to see the condition with an unjaundiced eye. What I have in mind is more like the Irish term *ag iompar clainne* (carrying a child), which is totally free of disguise and bias in its "unashamed frankness", a quality Yeats admired in early Irish verse. Such a quality also brings to mind Paulin's description of the "veracious abandon" of English vernacular verse (q.v.). However, I must stress that I am not claiming a state of non-bias for Irish at the expense of other languages. The term left-handed, *ciotóg*, for example, is equated with awkwardness in both English and Irish, and its equivalent in Spanish – *siniestro*, even has connotations of evil. Equally, it must be made clear that it is not euphemism or periphrasis in themselves that I am attacking, but rather how they can be used in a social context for the purpose of dissembling. As Leech points out (1969:140), periphrasis is frequently inherent in the beauty of a poetic utterance, for example, in *Romeo and Juliet*: "Night's candles are burnt out, and jocund day/stands tiptoe on the misty mountain tops..."

[3] In Robert James Waller's bestseller, *The Bridges of Madison County* (1993), such a bias is evident. Francesca Johnson is trying in vain to teach Yeats to an adolescent class: "But the bias against poetry they had picked up, the view of it as a product of unsteady masculinity was too much even for Yeats to overcome." When she read "the golden apples of the sun," one boy formed his hands as if to cup them over a woman's breasts, and the boys sniggered and the girls blushed. Waller sums up the unwritten code when he writes of Francesca's reaction

> They would live with those attitudes all their lives. That's what had discouraged her, knowing that, and she felt compromised and alone, in spite of the outward friendliness of the community. Poets were not welcome here (p.60).

By way of contrast, Adrienne Rich (1986) seems to have encountered shades of Vico on her visit to Nicaragua, where she was told: "You'll love Nicaragua: everyone there is a poet." Poetry there is uncloseted, celebratory and seen as a vehicle for personal immortality. She cites this as an example of what art means in a country uncontaminated by capitalism. Her perception (p.167) of the predominant attitude towards poetry in the U.S. is that it is not taken seriously, but rather treated as a "decorative garnish on the buffet table of the university curriculum".

5 SEEING SIGNS

As Santoro-Brienza points out (1993:27), the mind was born out of semiosis, i.e., seeing an object as something different to itself: the stone on a beach as a flint; the branch as a weapon; the fur as clothing; the word as the concept. When Hermes saw the tortoise as a lyre and thus transformed him, art was born. Art is therefore a "metamorphosis into form by violation" (p.6).

Santoro-Brienza describes a work of art as "a sign of the real, of the ideal, of the possible, of the utopic image of a more perfect, spiritual world" (p.27). However, he is quick to point out that artistic signs differ from ordinary signs in that they are self-referential and polysemic.[1] Thus art affords us the opportunity to challenge and to violate quotidian and routine ways of perceiving the world.

Hawkes (1977:144) argues, that in proportion to the decline in a belief and ultimate objective reality and order in the universe, it follows that there has to be a corresponding increase in the significance of our sign system, as a way of interpreting the thus fragmented nature of our worlds. He singles out poetry in particular, not only for its aesthetic, but also for its semiotic and interpretative insights into many aspects of existence. By recognising that a poem is not a window on established reality (cf. perspectivism, q.v.), it "can be identified as a sign system in its own right, with its own properties and its own distinct character" (p.146).

There are many signs such as allegory, symbol, metonymy, synecdoche, used by poets to express their vision of the world, but none is as powerful as metaphor.[2] By means of metaphor the poet can create his own grammar and unlock his perceptions of reality to us. While metaphors are pervasive in everyday speech (Pollio {1977} estimates that most speakers of English utter 3,000 novel metaphors per week), overuse leads to their diminution in effectiveness. They become clichés (e.g. "time flies," "spill the beans" etc.) and are frozen in language. However, the role of metaphor in acts of cognition cannot be underestimated. Skinner (1957) included metaphor in an overall theory of human verbal behaviour. Winner (1982) makes a greater claim for metaphor by stating that it constitutes the only means by which certain topics can be verbalised, and that communication would be severely curtailed if people were limited to strictly literal language. Hence the importance of poetry to rejuvenate our images and metaphors when they become worn-out or embedded for long periods in prose.

The eighteenth century Italian philosopher Vico (q.v.) was one of the first to propose metaphor as a more effective way of expressing abstract thought than mere literal language: "When we give utterance to our understanding of spiritual things, we must seek aid from our imagination to explain them and, like painters, form human images of them" (Bergin & Fish, 1984:402). As Danesi (1985:527) points out: "metaphor allows humans to interact with the environment, and to transform the outside world into an inner world of meaning."

In the light of frozen metaphors and clichés, what constitutes a good metaphor? Mininni (1989) posits the idea that the descriptive power of a metaphor is determined by the admissibility of its opposite. i.e., it endures the inversion of its grounds according to a higher logic of reciprocity (p.245), e.g. "to be born is to arrive a little" can be reversed simply: "to arrive is to be born a little." This can lead the mind further to reverse opposites, e.g. "to die is to depart a little". Such inversion, he argues, shows "the validity of the opposite link". For example, if you extol the beauty of your wife "one can show you the intrusive presence of your mother-in-law" (p.245). A speaker holds power by using metaphor. It is an extra tool (and, as has already been mentioned, in some cases the only tool) to elucidate his point of view. If one considers this in the light of the poet who coins his own metaphors, his position as a communicator should be very powerful indeed.

Metaphor is a fundamental mechanism of semiotic creativity. "This figure of speech mediates a sign and its referent through a signification process which causes the receiver of the overt signal to fill in a meaning" (Nuessel, 1989:245). Mukarovsky (1977:69) claims that poetic language is the negation of literal language: just as the *signifiant* and *signifie* of Saussure's sign form the recto and verso of a sheet of paper, so the aesthetic function is "the dialectic negation of every practical function".

Thus it can be argued that metaphor, by positing a new way of seeing, actually creates rather than simply represents new aspects of reality. It is worth considering this in the light of the Sapir-Whorf hypothesis (Whorf, 1978), which maintains that users of different grammars can arrive at somewhat different views of the world. Our linear conception of time[3] in the Western world seems to conflict with our abstract and spiritual thinking (cf. Bergson, q.v.). Whorf's study of how the Hopi Indians conceive time, space and matter (p.148 et seq.) is illuminating in the context of poetic thought, offering as it does, an alternative way of constructing reality. The Hopi practise meditative preparedness (cf. Wordsworth, q.v.), and intensity of thinking in anticipation of events in their lives (e.g. a harvest or a wedding), believing that readiness will improve the happening. By looking into the Hopi world, we soon realise that we make too many assumptions in English, as if they were totally logical; for example, nouns like summer and morning are phase terms in Hopi (p.143); or when we are thirsty, instead of asking for water or tea, we ask for a glass of water, or a cup of tea, i.e., we use the name of containers, when what we really mean are the contents. The Hopi on the other hand, will ask for "a water" (p.141); or when we look upon the process of cooling as the removal of heat, to the Hopi, it is seen as the addition of cold (p.251). As Whorf maintains, "alienness often turns into a new and clarifying way of looking at things" (p.264).

Perhaps if we were to don the Hopi mantle, the meaning of poetry would come more easily to us.[4] Art does not simply represent the world, but presents creative insights into it, and if we look upon metaphor as an alternative way of seeing, we will realise the vital role it has to play, not only in our understanding of poetry, but also in finding meaning to our lives.

NOTES

[1] In literal language, also, words can of course have more than one meaning. In poetry such meanings are multiplied even more, and rendered more complex. Such is the ambiguity in many poems, that their signifiers become swamped by their signfieds until both are one. Eagleton (1983:102) summarises the process

> Each sign participates in several different paradigmatic patterns or systems simultaneously, this complexity is greatly compounded by the syntagmatic chains of association, the lateral rather than vertical structures in which signs are placed.

And it is this complexity and ambiguity which alter the structural role of the sign from that of signifier to that of signified.

[2] Metaphor distinguishes itself from other tropes, according to Rice and Schofer (1981:108), in that it involves, not only substitution, but also transfer of meaning. Metonymy, synecdoche and irony are deterministic and limiting in the choices offered to the reader, e.g. part for a whole: "give me a hand," i.e., physical help; cause for effect: "I read Joyce," i.e., his works. Besides, such tropes are firmly anchored to the two basic elements of literature: narration and description. Esnault (1964:177) points out that metonymy

> does not open new paths like metaphorical intuition, but taking too familiar paths in its stride, it shortens distances so as to facilitate the swift intuition of things already known.

Metaphor, on the other hand, based on association and with only one shared semantic feature (among many found in two words) needed to establish a relationship, allows the reader much more freedom of selection." If in Freudian terms, for example, we were to equate sword with penis, then, as Rice and Schofer point out (P.9)

> at this point, rhetorical decoding becomes part of interpretation, an activity that takes place when the reader does not just consider the signs of the text at face value, but also exploits the (free) associations that a word or group of words provide.

[3] Part of the pseudo-rationality – the hubris – of modernity, is due to its impoverished grasp of relevant time. In Hopi, for example, there are no words to refer to time. It is perceived as a continuum. Our capitalist-orientated world, however, is centred around linear and metronomic time – depreciation charges, insurance premiums, pensions etc. Considering time as a tape measure, according to Whorf, leads to monotony. By routinising and giving us a false sense of security (anaesthetising us, as it were), it deprives us of the foresight to protect ourselves against hazards (p.154). We are relatively uninterested in stopping energy from causing fires (Whorf was a fireman), explosions etc. In a society as small as Hopi, however, such events would be disastrous.

[4] I am not suggesting that Hopi is a poetical language; in fact, according to Whorf (p.146), it contains no spatial metaphors. I am simply citing it as an example of an alternative way of looking at the world, something which poetry also attempts to do, but mainly through metaphor.

6 SEEING GRAMMATICALLY

6.1 TWO THEORIES

6.1.1 Jakobson's Theory

Following Valéry's definition of literature as "a kind of extension and application of certain properties of language" (Culler, 1975:55), Roman Jakobson (1960) attempted to apply the techniques of structural linguistics to the language of poems. Jakobson was critical of those who analysed language solely as semiotic, pointing out that language fulfils six functions: the referential, the emotive, the phatic, the conative, the metaphysical and the poetic, and none of these can be omitted if a comprehensive theory of language is to be achieved.

In poetry, we pay attention to equivalences in the process of combining words together, as well as in selecting them. Words which are semantically, rhythmically or phonetically equivalent are linked because of similarities, oppositions or parallels created by their sound, meaning, rhythm or connotations. As Jakobson puts it (p.358): "The poetic function projects the principle of equivalence from the axis of selection into the axis of combination."[1] By thus placing together in sequence patterns that are similar, and by processes of

elimination, we can fathom the "masterly interplay of actualised constructions".
He compares the juxtaposition of contrasting grammatical categories in poetry to
"dynamic cutting" in film montage, which is done, in order to generate ideas in
the minds of spectators, that the sequences do not carry by themselves.

6.1.2 Levin's Theory

Seeing poetry in terms of equivalence or parallelism was extended by Samuel
Levin (1962) with his theory of *Couplings*.[2] Borrowing heavily on Saussure, by
trying to unite *in praesentia* what otherwise would be united *in absentia*, he holds
that when equivalents are set in position in the syntagms, we have poetic
coupling, and it is this type of coupling which serves to fuse form and meaning in
a poem. In Pope's line: "A soul as full of Worth as void of Pride," "Pride" and
"Worth" are coupled. They are set in strict grammatical relation, and display
structural correspondence; "full" and "void" are antonyms. Therefore it follows,
that "Worth/Pride", since they are positionally equivalent, must also be antonyms.

   Another function of coupling, he maintains, is to make poems memorable,
rhyme being a mnemonic aid. Thus, while "ordinary language" fades, the form
and impression of the poem remain permanently in the mind.

6.1.3 Seeing Structural Crevices

Such theories have certain merits: they demystify language; they help us to gain
flexibility in verbal skills, and enrich our semantic and syntactic codes. However,
they fail in a number of ways: Levin's idea of memorability is negated by many
modern poems, which ignore obvious or mnemonic sound patterns. Both theorists
seem to view a poem as a mechanical construction, which is alien to the
spontaneous, aleatory and "irrational" nature of creativity, alluded to in Chapter 2.
Jakobson's quests for patterns, in an attempt to establish a comprehensive,

linguistic theory of poetry, are frequently erroneous. Jonathan Culler (1975) shows convincingly how Jakobson's applied theory to Shakespeare's one hundredth and twenty ninth sonnet ("Th'expense of spirit was a waste of shame") was a misinterpretation (p.72), and points out, that if a linguist proposes meanings which the poet did not intend, then it is the linguist who is at fault.[3] Jakobson subordinates theme to language, instead of it being the other way round. As Culler points out: "One should start with effects, and then see how grammatical structures contribute to account for those effects" (p.73). In other words by interpreting a poem purely grammatically, one could lose or misinterpret its meaning.[4] Or as Barthes (1967) perceives it: the linguist, by failing to take into account the multiplicity of factors, rational and irrational, that contribute to the reading of a poem, sometimes "discovers the flower, but not the bouquet".

Even the paradigmatic system itself is fallible (see note[1]), as Bruner (p.23) illustrates, by quoting MacNeice's (1949)

> The sunlight on the garden
> Hardens and grows old
> We cannot cage the minute
> Within its nets of gold

as an example of metaphorical ambiguity, non-amenable to a selection and substitution theory, based on literal transference. (To what does "sunlight on the garden" refer? Or "hardens" in such a context etc?). Art, in its subversive role, can ignore obvious combinations and theory altogether, and this, according to Bruner (p.23), is

> where poetry rises up above ordinary language. This is where its strength lies in its ungraspability, its defiance of obvious automatic transference, and it is this very characteristic that enables it to make the world newly strange.

NOTES

[1] In Jakobson there is a hierarchy of combinations: phonemes, for example are combined according to rules at the next level, i.e., morphemes, which in turn combine with lexemes, and so on to sentences and discourse. Thus one does not study any single level on its own, but selects and combines vertically (paradigmatically) and horizontally (syntagmatically). The vertical substitution is usually by way of a literal synonym, but can also be metaphorical: *girl – maiden – flower*. Horizontal substitutions are more problematic in that, being predicative (*the girl wept oceans*), they often involve truth functions supported by metaphor, rendering them strange or vague, and thus difficult to replicate (cf. MacNeice's *Sunlight on the Garden, q.v.*).

[2] For a different angle on *Couplings*, consider Octavio Paz's sexual couplings of words (as in *Salamandra*,{1962}), in order to produce new, fertilised meanings.

[3] It is understandable, if in some respects, this is seen as a moot point. For example, if one considers a poem in a Barthian context, or in the light of reception theory, then it takes on a life of its own, thus lacking an authorial or authoritative voice. One has only to consider, in this light, Johnson's "correction" of Goldsmith's "misinterpretation" of his own poem (Stanford:118); or Dylan Thomas' exegetic dispute with a reader of his poetry (Leech:49); or the annoyance of Tennyson on not being understood (cf. Ch.11). An aspect of the beauty of art lies in its polysemy, and its ultimate test, surely, rests in the meaning which moves one the most. However, a wariness is needed of those who approach a poem from a narrow standpoint (cf. Note⁴ below, & Ch.5).

[4] Does one drive a motor car to discover how the engine works? Or as Paz (1970) put it, in relation to myths: "if the speaker of a language were to conscientiously apply the rules of grammar to his speech, he would lose the thread of what he wanted to say."

7 SEEING BETWEEN TEXTS

7.1 Seeing Palimpsests

Intertextuality was a term coined by Julia Kristeva (1986) to refer to the non-independence of any text. According to her, both reader and writer (who is a reader also) bring to the text other texts and influences which affect their interpretation of it. These become subtexts[1] in their analysis. An interesting proposition here (in keeping with Barthes' idea of "death of the author")[2] is the consideration of the role of the creator of the text as merely an instrument. For example, some references in the work may be dormant to the writer but not to the reader, and so the latter has an active role of "aggressive participation" (Kristeva) in helping to co-create the work.

This idea, however, has been adopted by some literary critics as a *carte blanche* to complete the work, as it were, for the author. While interpretation is to be welcomed, there can be danger in this type of activity, especially if one approaches the text from a narrow standpoint. It can lead to misinterpretation, as we have already mentioned in relation to Jakobson's analysis of a Shakespearean sonnet.

Nevertheless, there can be no doubt that texts are based on other texts. A simple example: Larkin's *Born Yesterday*, contains echoes of two literary precursors: the subtle echo of Pope's mock-heroic style: "without sneering/Teach the rest to sneer" (*Epistle to Dr. Arbuthnot*), can be found in Larkin's wish for the newly-born girl (Sally Amis) that she may not be endowed with beauty, which "unworkable itself/Stops all the rest from working". However, the more obvious subtext lies in Yeats' *Prayer for My Daughter*

> May she be granted beauty and yet not
> Beauty to make a stranger's eye distraught
> Or hers before a looking-glass...

which Larkin renders

> May you be ordinary...
> Not ugly, not good-looking
> Nothing uncustomary
> To pull you off your balance.[3]

We have referred earlier to precursor texts as palimpsests, upon which new texts try to impress themselves (Ch. 4.2). This could explain, to some degree at least, the reason why some creative writers read other texts in such great quantities: it is perhaps with the hope of inducing a creative explosion, as it were, on their part. It is as if the ingesting of others' works overloads the writer's brain, so that his own work has to be forced out on to the paper or word processor.

Intertextuality, particularly when transcultural (why should anyone be confined to the art of one country?), can be quite illuminating in helping us to understand poetry in a wider and consequently richer context.[4] We have already mentioned the "panther" behind bars in the Austrian poet Rilke. How similar he is to the caged "tiger" in the Mexican Ruvalcaba, or the Polish Milosz' "tiger," or even Blake's English "tyger". All poets become one poet, as it were, in ascribing a terrifying, creative power to their animal-symbol.

7.2 Crying for the Moon

I would like to conclude this chapter by considering for a moment the role of the moon – the symbol of poetic vulnerability – intertextually and as a transcultural symbol; also, how it is perceived similarly by modern poets of different cultures, and in a way quite differently from their predecessors; and finally, in so doing, to attempt to interpret their message for modern society.

The moon was for centuries perceived by poets as a pure poetic symbol, always pristine in its inspiration: "La luna en el mar riela" ("The moon glimmers on the sea") as Espronceda put it traditionally.[5] However, the modern poet sees the moon as tarnished, as something that has been defiled by modern man, and it is interesting that this view is held transculturally. One could observe the moon in modern poetry as a barometer on the condition of the world. Let us look briefly at how three modern poets, Paz, Lowell and Lorca perceive the moon.

In Paz's poem *Salamandra* (1962), the moon has been violated by the world and "como un borracho cae de bruces" ("like a drunkard falls on its face") and "los carniceros se lavan las manos en el agua de la luna" ("butchers wash their hands in the moon's water"). Paz sees the *Salamandra* as a criticism of language, criticising the cliché-ridden word, until he finds its pristine meaning – origins, mother, salt, water etc., and thus liberates himself from the contaminating effects of history (Wilson, 1986).

Lowell, in *Fall 1961*, senses our end drifting nearer, and "the moon lifts,/radiant with terror". The moon gauges our condition, and "We are like a lot of wild/spiders crying together,/but without tears".

The moon is pervasive in Lorca's poetry, particularly in *Poeta en Nueva York*, where it represents wounded nature: "y algún perfil de yeso tranquilo que dibuja/instantáneo dolor de luna apuntillada" ("and some profile of peaceful plaster which draws/the instant pain of the punctured moon"). The anxiety in "the sad fossil world," which Lorca saw all round him in New York is reminiscent of

Paz, as he fails to find "el acento de su primer sollozo"("the accent of its first sob").

The poet's concerns are not just about his own country, and the wounded moon is a modern beacon for all climes.

NOTES

[1] Subtexts, as Tammi (1991) points out, are very valuable for solving hermeneutic problems in literary texts. She sets out to prove her theory by applying the Taranovsky method (similar to an extension of Jakobson's poetic function), to the field of intertextuality. She cites Taranovsky (p.320), who points out that the juxtaposition of one text with another necessarily produces more poetic information. She also, rather interestingly, avers that intertextuality, as a process, may also be retroactive, in that our reading of a later text may influence our perception of a previous one. Such a phenomenon, she maintains, is due to changes which occur in the conventions of reading itself, and in accordance with the demands set by new and innovative texts (p.325). One could add that changing societal expectations could also have an impact on such a process (cf. the different approaches to productions of Shakespeare's plays {both theatrical and filmic} since the author first penned them).

[2] Texts are fragments by definition in open and endless relation with all other texts. No one text therefore is self-sufficient. Each one is like an entry in a encyclopaedia, referring parenthetically to other references, except, as Regueiro Elam points out: "there is no way to contain all possible references in any encyclopedic 'whole'" (Princeton:621). On this basis, it may be argued, that no writer can ever be in control of the meaning of the text. Thus the traditional meaning of author – in the sense of one with authority – now becomes suspect (cf. Ch.6:N).

[3] Larkin's poetry, in its turn, can also act as palimpsest: In Heaney's *Digging*: "Between my finger and my thumb/The squat pen rests...," there are both thematic and verbal resonances of Larkin's *Toads*: "Why should I let the toad *work*/Squat on my life?"

[4] Intertextuality enables us to see tradition, not as a succession of happenings, but as system of significant relations. For example, Peter Levi (1991) in his *Art of Poetry* jumps with synchronic felicity from Horace to Pasternak to Auden and back again, in an illuminating study of their poetry and their relations to each other, without limiting them in any way historically.

[5] While in Western mythology the moon was perceived as a repository of unfulfilled desires (Brewer, 1990:745), the Chinese attached even more importance to it, seeing it as the source of being itself: the verb "to be" in Chinese means literally "to snatch from the moon with the hand".

8 THE COMPOUND EYE

One effect of intertextual studies was that it tended to erase former disciplinary boundaries, so that subjects such as philosophy, psychoanalysis and science all entered the fray as discursive practices (as indeed had been the case with all knowledge up to the Age of Reason).[1] Besides, why should the many disciplines of knowledge hide away from each other in dark corridors, when they could possibly achieve so much more heuristically by coming together? (cf. Ch.3:N[1]).

Umberto Eco (1989:39) maintains that aesthetics in itself is unable to give an exhaustive explanation of itself, and thus recommends the value of calling on the assistance of psychology, sociology, anthropology and other sciences in a common hermeneutic. Furthermore, science itself is no longer viewed as a paragon of objectivity, or of having a monopoly over knowledge, and indeed, according to many people, it fails to satisfy emotionally. So why not pool resources? In fact, science has more in common with art than it sometimes likes to believe. For example, where does reason fit into the many inventions and discoveries which are the products of the "irrational" world of dreams?[2]

Ian Milner, in his introduction to the poetry of the scientist-poet, Miroslav Holub (1990:13), sees a connection between the scientific method and poetry-making: He maintains that looking into a microscope and "seeing the expected (or at times the unexpected but meaningful)" is similar to looking at the "nascent organism of the poem". As Holub puts it

> Here too are cemeteries,
> fame and snow.
> And I hear murmuring:
> the revolt of immense estates.
> (*In the Microscope*)

When Plato banished the poets from his ideal republic for being irrational,[3] he missed a vital point. He presumed the world could be contained within a system of logic, and consequently failed to deal adequately with man in his completeness i.e., as a combination of rational and irrational forces (cf. Freud, q.v.). Man has an unconscious affinity with the four elements: earth, air, fire, water, and expresses values which persist, despite the evidence of reason (Jones, 1990).

The French philosopher and scientist Gaston Bachelard tried to free irrationality from its pejorative connotations. The mathematical symbol Π, he pointed out, originally in his doctoral thesis (1928), is incapable of being reduced to a whole number; therefore it cannot he known exactly. This led him to his theory of *Approximates*. To admit the incompleteness of knowledge is to him a sign, not of failure, but of objectivity (cf. Peirce's principle of *Fallibilism*, {Berthoff, 1991:138}).[4] By relating the rational to the nonrational, in other words by combining science and poetry, and having an openness of approach, we can widen our conception of reality. As Jones (p.160) puts it

> Consciousness for Bachelard is against a complex, hostile reality and against its own past, too, its rational past: ideas must be endlessly rectified, for what was thought to be true is shown to be false or incomplete, imprecise.

This is also in keeping with Lacan's point that language is ambiguous and that we can never really say what we mean, or mean precisely what we say. Meaning is "an approximation, a near-miss, a part failure" (Eagleton:169).

The Cartesian "I think, therefore I am," for Bachelard, becomes "I think therefore I evolve" (Jones:160) i.e., I think against a complex reality and become a complex being.[5]

Bachelard attempts to present a new understanding of imaginary consciousness by relating subject and object in the image of poetry. In *Imagination and Reverie* (1971:6), he sees poetry as the "intermediate" zone of consciousness, "the zone of reveries" that precedes contemplation. Seeing imagination in such an open way, led him to differ with F. R. Leavis in his interpretation of Shelley's *Ode to the West Wind* Leavis is quite critical of this poem, believing that it is not a work of active intelligence. Bachelard, on the other hand, considers Shelley to be a "true poet", and believes, that by accepting the poem as it is, the reader's imagination is opened through it to the forces of the cosmos (Jones:166).

While life's normal activities can be described in prose quite adequately, Bachelard believes that poetry is necessary to get at the hidden sources of our psyches. According to him, poetic images are (in Jones' translation) "elevation operators". They raise us up and fill us with a desire to grow. For Bachelard, the chief function of poetry is to "transform us". This is achieved on the part of the reader by being in a state of open imagination (cf. Ch.1), so that he can continue the writer's images, and thus enrich his own consciousness, which is ever-changing.

If what we perceive as the world is not something immutable, but as Bruner (p.105) puts it, as something that is merely a "stipulation couched in a symbol system"

> then the shape of the discipline alters radically. And we are, at last, in a position to deal with the myriad forms that reality can take – including the realities created by story, as well as those created by science.

NOTES

[1] As Hawkes (1977:8) points out (and notwithstanding our criticisms in Ch.5), the Saussurean linguistic model provides a basis for the study of knowledge in its totality (cf. Levi-Strauss' application of Saussure's principles to anthropology). Thus it is necessary to refer to other disciplines when examining art, to see how the various parts relate to the whole (cf. Eco, q.v.).

[2] The chemist August Kekule's dream – in the form of a snake swallowing its own tail – provided the solution to the nature of the benzene ring (Gregory:172) (cf. Ch.2:N[1]).

[3] "The imitative poet implants an evil constitution, for he indulges the irrational nature which has no discernment of greater or less" (Plato, *The Republic*: x).

[4] Such a theory could also help to break down the metalanguage of science as a dogma of non-variance, which, unlike poetry, does not allow for alternatives.

[5] Sadly, "the complex being" of adulthood has the effect of incarcerating rather than liberating us. A child, for example, does not distinguish between literal or metaphorical language in linguistic acquisition. It was probably such a realisation that prompted Wordsworth to exclaim that the child is the "first poet" (cf. Vico). In Blake's *Songs of Innocence*, the child is happy recounting the pleasures of nature, but in *Songs of Experience*, he is trapped and confused by human institutions (cf. what Ossian foresaw in his *Colloquy* with Patric). Thus it is not surprising to confront the common motif of longing for a return to childhood in the work of many poets, most notably that of Wordsworth, Blake, and the Gaelic poet, Máirtín Ó Direáin.

9 SEEING CLEARANCES

While free verse is not a recent phenomenon (Whitman's *Leaves of Grass* {1855} bears witness to that fact), nevertheless the fragmentation of much of society, which occurred after two world wars, gave an added impetus to its more widespread use. Closed structures could no longer hold sway. Adorno's famous quotation that "after Auschwitz, to write lyric poetry is barbaric" (Rich, 1974:141), meant that poetry could never again be conceived merely as a self-indulgent or complacent act.

Barthes' "death of author" (1967), Lyotard's "little narratives" (1984), and Vattimo's *pensiore debole* or "weak thought" (1988)[1] all joined in an attempt to free the world from the power of traditional metaphysics and the destructive hegemonies of the past.

Western language was perceived as enclosing and inhibiting, placing barriers between the individual and reality. Truth lies with the poets, but only if they break from linearity[2] (cf. Vico), and the reification of the enclosed poem, or when, as Austin Clarke points out: "they take the clappers from the bell of rhyme" (Heaney, 1988:9). Poet and reader must be brought closer together by a freer verse. Even the word stanza originally meant a room, and when embracing metre, rhyme etc., suggests incarceration of thought with its formal rules of grammar. As Tomlinson (1972) puts it

Man in an interior, sits down
Before an audience of none.
He is biding his time for the rhymes
That will arise at the threshold of his mind
Pass words into the castle keep,
The city of sleepers. Wakened by him
Stanza by stanza (room by room)
They will take him sleeper in.
(*The Demise of the Modern Poet*)

Bradford (1993:165), cites Auden's poem on Brueghel's painting, *The Fall of Icarus* (cf. Ch.10), as an example, where the poet defies the logic of conventional grammar, as he takes personal control (rather than submit to convention) over the nature of his own linguistic material

the sun shone
As it had to on the white legs disappearing into the green water.

Bradford (p.165) points out that, as we witness the boy's white legs disappearing into the green of the painting, "we realise the materiality of language is being used to create an effect very similar to that achieved with the materials of visual art".

Poetry must be seen as a natural act, with pauses coming as we breathe (cf. Ginsberg's *Howl* {1956}, and later *Moloch*: "Experience is a deluge no form can contain" {Perkins, 1987:346}). Such subversion of form is atavistic, in that it recalls primitive man's first engagement with the natural world, by means of physical responses. In free verse we are allowed to share in a *parole* with the poet listening to his own words gambolling on a page, which are free from the shackles of enforced grammar.

Nevertheless, *vers libre* does not necessarily mean a total abandonment of rhyme or order ("playing tennis with the nets down," as Robert Frost described it {Winokur, 1987:82}). However, the impetus for its use now becomes more textural than textual, more as instances than as part of an overall design.

Otherwise, we could be faced with the Hugo Williams' (1988) (admittedly ludic) problem, where composition is perceived as uncontrolled ejaculation

> Ten, no five seconds
> after coming all
> over the place
> too soon
> I was lying there
> wondering
> where to put the
> line-breaks in.

Vers libre also became popular with many women poets, who saw it as an opportunity of liberating themselves from the restrictions and stereotyping, which they suffered under patriarchal language. Even T.S. Eliot (1953:91) had to admit that with "rhyme forbidden, many Shagpats were unwigged". As Montefiori (1983:76) points out: "correct English blanks out realities it has no room for" (cf. John Clare, q.v.). Injustices are encoded into its structure. The term "free verse" itself was initially derogatory (Princeton:425). Adrienne Rich's *The Burning of Paper instead of Children* (1974), employs the "incorrectness" of an immigrant's words, not only to highlight injustice, but also to guarantee their authenticity

> ... a child did not had dinner last night: a child steal because he did not have money to buy it: to hear a mother say she do not have food for her children and tosee a child without cloth it will make tears in your eyes.

Thus free verse deautomatises our reading; it yields pleasures in its unpredictability; it tries to replicate lived experience; it makes words – even "lowly prepositions" (Princeton:427) stand out more as material entities. Let us now examine some of the more experimental nature of free verse in William Carlos Williams, e e cummings, et al., as we turn our gaze towards visual poetry.

NOTES

[1] Vattimo proposes "weak thought" as the only way of loosening the stranglehold of the metaphysical tradition. Advocating a form of positive nihilism, he proposes a gradual wearing down and dissection of all claims to universal or hegemonic truths. The influence of Nietzsche is evident ("Nihilism stands at the door") in his assertion that "truths" such as God and the Soul can be revealed to be no less "errors" (p.xii) than any other belief system. In a similar way Lyotard's "little narratives are posited as multi-tiered discourses on society, in direct opposition to a totalising world metanarrative; and Barthes' "death of author" is also an anti-authoritarian device to open the text to a more readerly and polysemic approach (cf. Ch.5:N & Ch.6:N).

[2] In a parallel fashion, prose fiction was also attempting to break free from grammatical and ethical restrictions, as evidenced by the "stream of consciousness" techniques of modernist writers such as James Joyce and Virginia Woolf.

10 THE DESPOTISM OF THE EYE

10.1 Erect Irises

Just as we have shown that free verse is not a recent phenomenon, neither is visual poetry, if one considers it in the context of Blake's eidetic imagery, coupled with his drawings and paintings, or Apollinaire's *calligrammes*, which were literary counterparts of Cubist innovations. The beauty of the visual form of an object has long been known as having a selling impact. The design of a book containing poems – often with a copy of a painting on its jacket – can act as an attractive enticer to unfold the cover and see the print style, the lay-out, the quality of paper etc., all of which have an aesthetic role to play in influencing its purchase. In this context also, consider the subliminal, proselytising impact of gold-edged bibles and missals in beautiful print, and covered in vellum (a legacy of monastic scribes).

However, as Bradford informs us, the publication of William Carlos Williams' *Spring and All*, and e e cummings' *Tulips and Chimneys*, both in 1923, "signalled the emergence of visual form as a phenomenon that could rescue the post-traditional poem from the dangers of interpretative displacement" (p.88). The jolting effects of visual shapes are like original metaphors of a pre-linguistic experience. With – what Lynne Tillman (1991) calls, in another context –

"erect irises" we can see clearly again through humbug and hypocrisy. When this visualisation is combined with Vattimo's et al (q.v.) iconoclastic ideas, it can have a powerful impact. Consider the visual attempt by cummings to reduce God, America and the ego by minisculisation in the poem, whose first line is the hyperbaton: "next to of course god america" (Hawkes, 1977:138).

As technology became more complex in modern society, some poets responded with greater experimentation, which sometimes led to the creation of poems that can never be spoken. Consider the following poem by William Carlos Williams (Perkins, 1987:260), which attempts to capture an aspect of a metropolitan world, in its description of an advertisement in neon lights

```
* * *
* S *
* O *
* D *
* A *
* * *
```

It is interesting to point out that the impact of such a poem is greater, when displayed on a phosphorescent VDU, than as unilluminated print on a page.

Or reflect on the following, by Eugen Gomringer (Solt, 1968:92), as a parody on the paradox of mimesis

```
ping  pong
   ping  pong  ping
   pong  ping  pong
      ping  pong
```

Ping does not accurately represent the sound of a bouncing ball. We pretend it does, as *moo* represents the sound of a cow, or *mioew* the sound of a cat, which is in keeping with Saussure's dictum on the arbitrariness of the sign (q.v.). Thus all mimetic efforts are merely approximations, and sometimes problematic (cf. Tennyson's failed onomatopoeic rendition {Ch. 11}). The above "poem" is an attempt at visual onomatopoeia, where, as Bradford informs us (p.132), "the signifiers seem to be literally bouncing diagonally down the page before coming to a halt".

With the exception of performance poetry, and some oral attempts, which we shall examine later, the relationship between the modern poet and reader (q.v.) is mainly one of silence. Thus the reader is drawn to the physicality of the poem, which, as Bradford points out (p.67), makes the visual materiality of language the theme, as well as the functional condition of the poem. Consider the play on silence itself in Gomringer's concrete poem (Solt:91)

```
silencio  silencio  silencio
silencio  silencio  silencio
silencio            silencio
silencio  silencio  silencio
silencio  silencio  silencio
```

As Solt indicates, the absence in the third column of the poem is like the space frequently left by an abstract painting in an art gallery. The constant repetition of the single word is like a visual version of a mantra or, as we mentioned earlier, the Vedic, vibratory attempt to physically realise the world. However, the ludic element is also evident in such poetry and, according to Gomringer, it is designed to renew our sense of fun: the poet determines the play area and the reader grasps the idea of play and joins in (Solt:67).

However, as Bradford avers (p.133), words will always signal an intention to say something, despite concrete poetry, or the pursuit of silence by poets such as the Spaniard, Francisco Brines (1977) who "abre la boca y está mudo" ("opens his mouth and is mute"). However, like Samuel Beckett, Brines knows that he must "go on", and slither like a snake through the "huérfana noche" ("the orphan night"), to try to unravel some of the enigma of existence, because true silence can only be communicated by its absence.

Nevertheless, when one considers a world, where words are cheapened by their overuse, as in information technology, there is a case to be made at least for minimalism in language, as in the work of Beckett et al. It is interesting to consider that some cultures still revere the word. Maori women, for example, do not speak, but confine themselves to body language after a relative's death, and Papuan people, when in similar circumstances, remove several words from their language as a sign of mourning (Barthes, 1966:48). Human loss is also word loss for them, a communal admission that the diminishment of one reduces all.

When we reflect on the great pains that some people go to in order to communicate, perhaps more thought should be put into how words are used in our Western, consumer society. In this context also, I cite the remarkable courage of the severely brain-damaged Irish poet, Christopher Nolan, to communicate, by typing with a unicorn stick attached to his forehead.

Returning to the silence of concrete poetry, where one constructs a poem as it were, it is ironic that, rather than being a suave sophisticate, the concrete poem actually reflects the *verum factum* ("what I see I make") of primitive man, which is in keeping with Vico's view (q.v.) of our early ancestors as being naturally poetic. Also, the Greek conception of the poet as "maker", blends somewhat with Williams' view of the poem as a material thing,[1] perhaps like a house, where, as Eavan Boland (1994) hopes, "one can grow old in" (*A woman Painted on a Leaf*) (cf. Peter Levi's {1991} "we nest in our poem, we live in it").[2]

However, the visual is not always visionary[3] and sometimes content suffers for the sake of form. No matter how sophisticated a poem may appear, if it doesn't move us emotionally it has failed. Williams at times is over-indulgent in his creative playfulness. In *Perpetuum Mobile* and the *Corn Harvest*, both from *Pictures from Brueghel* (1962), he glides over issues, stereotyping girls as "silent or gabbing," or myopically seeing them in a sexist manner *en masse* as "they gather gossiping". Such verbal clichés are as bad as some of the formalist clichés which he tries to avoid. To borrow yet another cliché, one feels, that with Williams, it is sometimes a case of the kettle calling the pot black, especially when he decries modern poetics for a lack of base, which was something he himself helped to create. One is reminded of Hugo Williams' poem (op. cit.) in WCW's statement, that modern poetry "is all over the place at the mere whim of the man who has composed it" (Rosenthal, 1966:409).

10.2 Paint & Ink

Free verse enabled poetry to blend the temporal with the spatial. Instead of having to follow a poem in a linear way, it could now be observed all at once like a painting. This of course is not new to Chinese writing, which is ideogramatic and columnar. According to Fenollosa (1919), Chinese is superior to any Western language, in that it can represent images, metaphors and natural processes without having to have recourse to temporally confining grammar – verbs, adjectives, conjunctions etc. This is no small achievement for a language which was once only monosyllabic, and which has only 400 syllable sounds (Mac Leish, 1960:56).

The ideogram is like a continuous moving picture. Perhaps cummings' *Falling Leaf* (from *95 Poems*) is the nearest one can get to it in English

```
l (a)
le
af
fa
ll
s)
one
l
iness.
```

Here cummings, in a graphic vertical representation, tries to portray the leaf actually falling. As it falls, summer ends and one feels lonely. Silence has almost been reached here, and as Bradford points out (p.36), such a poetics is "capable of creating patterns of meaning far beyond its particular mimetic effect". The manner in which words are positioned on a page can alter our perception of linguistic meaning. As Forrest-Thompson (1978:40) affirms, visual poetry "brings out dormant elements in our prose".

Now, after the leaf-fall, it is appropriate to cite an attempt at visualising the wind

```
                    w    w
                 d    i
              n    n    n
           i    d    i    d
        w                 w
```

This poem by Gomringer (Solt:93) illustrates the arbitrary nature of language. It can be "read" along separate diagonal planes, and even along planes that are angular or curved. As Bradford explains (p.132)

> The meaning of such effects is presumably that in order to bring the arbitrary self-determined signifier closer to our experience of its referent, we might demonstrate how the components of this particular linguistic integer can be, literally blown around.

Quite a number of poets have tried to link poetry with painting (although ironically, cummings himself and D.H. Lawrence – both accomplished painters – kept their paintings and poems separate). It is also interesting to reflect that the reverse does not happen as often, i.e., painters turning to verse for artistic inspiration or fusion.[3] Both Auden and Williams were inspired by Brueghel, Eavan Boland by Degas, and Claudio Rodríguez by Velázquez, and Paul Durcan made an attempt with his art gallery poems, *Give Me Your Hand* (1994). According to Kathleen McCracken (1994:19), in her review of this work, Durcan "contemporises and localises content and context by means of irony, parody, idiom or allusion, and casts observation and judgement in the familiar form of a dramatic monologue or dialogue." McCracken argues, that by suggesting new or forgotten ways of seeing (by storytelling in a poetic narrative), Durcan is performing the true function of art – the giving of ourselves back to ourselves. To support her case, she cites Wim Wender's film *Wings of Desire* (1987), in which the old man, who is the guardian angel of the city of Berlin, says: "If mankind loses its storytellers, it loses its childhood."

On the other hand, Declan Kiberd (1991) adopts a more critical attitude towards Durcan in the main, saying that his style is "loose to the point of garrulity" (p.1398), but then goes on to modify this by asserting that such a style is really a deceptive mannerism. His is a style that works generally in the context of angst-ridden performance poetry. However, it doesn't lay claim to oral exclusivity, and some of it seems to look rather pedestrian when it hits print form. If to say much in little is the mark of great poetry, and repetitiveness is sometimes an indication of linguistic poverty (Leech:79), one is left to wonder if such prose poetry will stand the test of time. However, in his frequent onslaughts on politicians and clergy – sometimes humorous or even surreal – he does fill a satirical vacuum in modern Irish poetry.

Either way, we must retrace our steps a little to Claudio Rodríguez (1971) to witness an effort to fuse more than two art forms into one. In the poem *Hilando* (weaving), inspired by the painting *Las hilanderas* by Velázquez, when the weaver's blouse is compared to music, we witness the fusion of poetry, music and painting

> La camisa ya es música
> y está recién lavada/aclarada
> ("the blouse is music now
> having been just washed, made light")

As well as attempting to fuse art forms, words should appeal to as many senses[4] as possible, and the tactile is often a neglected aspect in poetry. Tomlinson's *A Meditation on John Constable*, attempts to write in "painterly" words

> Clouds
> Followed by others, temper the sun in passing

> Over and off it. Massed darks
> Blotting it back, scattered and mellowed shafts
> Break damply out of them...
>   It shrinks to a crescent
> Crushed out, a still lengthening ooze
>   As the mass thickens, though cannot exclude
> Its silvered-yellow.

Ink and paint blend into one, as they blot from the pen or ooze from the tube, and simultaneously darken the sun on canvas.

Eavan Boland's (1994) attempt to transform a mother's sorrow into a statue is reminiscent of the ancient Celtic story of Labhras Loinseach's barber, who unloaded his grief onto a tree, or of the fossilisation of sorrow in Shakespeare's Hermione (*The Winter's Tale*)

> the moment her sorrow entered marble
> the exact angle of the cut at which
> the sculptor made the medium remember
> its own ordeal in the earth, the aeons
> crushing and instructing it until it wept itself
> into inches, atoms of change.
> (*The Art of Grief*)

Such an attempt at an eternal synchronic entrapment of a moment in time also brings Keats' *Ode on a Grecian Urn* to mind: "Fair youth, beneath the trees, thou canst not leave/Thy song, nor ever can those trees be bare" (Hayward, 1956:295).

Visual form attempts to make poetry adapt to the modern age. While such efforts are laudatory and successful in their own way, one wonders, however, what price was paid for such a form, extolling, as it does, one sense above all the others.[5]

So let us turn our attention to another sense now: that of hearing, as we ask: what has poetry gained and lost by sacrificing so much of its sound?

NOTES

[1] But I don't subscribe to his branding of a poem as a "machine". Such. nomenclature ascribes a pejorative, technological quality (no matter how unwittingly) to a poem, which is the direct opposite to what poetry is all about (cf. Ch.12.)

[2] Contrarily, Brendan Kennelly believes 'it does no harm to feel homeless in a language. A language like any house can be a source of homely smugness' (Pierce, 2000:1106).

[3] There is ample evidence in modern urban society to give credence to the view that we have overstimulated one of our senses (the visual) at the expense of others. Even Walter Benjamin (1992:38) recognised the incipience of such a development in Baudelaire's time: "Interpersonal relationships in big cities are distinguished by a marked preponderance of the activity of the eye over the activity of the ear." Benjamin considered the new transportation systems (buses, trains, trams) as a major cause of this development, where people were forced to look at each other over a period of time, in close proximity and without speaking. In the contemporary era, one could argue that the condition has been exacerbated by the advent of TV, shopping malls, traffic signs, more sophisticated advertising, films, DVDs and computers.

[4] A discovered exception on my part to this tendency is to be found in the work of the Antrim-born artist Josephine Hardiman, who exhibited at the 1995 Hopkins Summer School. She made use of poetic extracts from Hopkins, Plath and Desmond Egan, not merely for inspirational purposes, but as intrinsic components of the works themselves.

[5] I wish to clarify here the distinction between the single, physical sense of sight, and "seeing" as I use it in the title and throughout this work. In the latter case it is meant as a blanketing term, to embrace all the physical senses, in addition to the enlightenment and spirituality achieved from inner vision. It is interesting to note that if we were to follow ancient teaching on the soul (Ecclus, xvii, 5), we would refer to seven and not five senses, man being influenced by the seven planets. Fire *animates*, earth gives the sense of *feeling*, water gives *speech*, air gives *taste*, mist gives *sight*, flowers give *hearing*, and the south wind gives *smelling* (Brewer:1004) (cf. Note[3]).

11 SEEING VOICES

11.1 A Sense of Loss

We have already praised minimalism in a world swamped by information, but are we missing out on the earliest-known quality of poetry itself – that of sound, produced by spent air, carbon dioxide, "the most wonderful by-product ever created" (Britannica, 10, 1977:648)? Despite its denigration by some poets, is poetry not losing out on one of its most emotive qualities by abandoning sound? Should our language not reflect, in Corman's words (1977:150) "the perceptions, urges, habits and rhythms of the body in its interaction with the natural world"? Should our poetry not be as natural as our breathing? By ignoring the sound, content are we amputating one of our senses? What of our song rhythms? Are we interring the "miracle of being" in a cement culture? Ruth Underhill, commenting on Papago songs, claimed that they make Indians visualise the eagle, which, in their belief system, is sacred and superior to man. Through the intercession of the songs, the eagle will cleanse the world from disease and even ward off death (Princeton:77). And all this is done through sound. It seems we have lost our way in the Western world, and all our incantations have dried up.

What specifically have we lost? Tom Paulin (1990) argues that we have lost the greater freedom and "veracious abandon" (p.xvi) which characterised vernacular verse at the expense of the more censorious written standard. To support his point, he quotes from the anonymous *A Pitman's Lovesong* (p.xvi)

> Aw wish my lover was a ripe turd
> smoking doon in yon dyke seid
> an aw mysel was a shitten flee
> aw'd sook her allup before she was dreid

Fiona Pitt-Kethley illustrates such difficulties in print form, in her parodic poem *Censorship* (Ricks, 1990:422)

> The BBC does not like certain words.
> Dildoes and buggery are always out.
> "Cocks are OK, as long as they aren't sucked"
> a young researcher telephoned me back.

It is the poet alone, according to Baudelaire, who "comprehends the universal analogy", something which makes poetic imagination the "most scientific of all the faculties" (Macleish:69) (cf. Ch.8). Thus, as we have mentioned earlier, poetry cannot sidestep taboo areas, for to do so, would be to betray "the universal analogy", which, according to MacLeish, is something censors continually fail to understand.

Paulin (1992) also illustrates how increasing standardisation of the written word has led to the loss of great dialectical riches. He cites John Clare, the "peasant poet", whose rich dialect words were seen as deviant,[1] and were standardised by his publisher, who imposed a grammar, which tended to suffocate the spontaneity of his verse. Thus we are not surprised when Clare exclaims that "grammar in learning is like tyranny in government" (p.53) (cf. St. Paul's fear of the impact of the severity of his letters[2]). His unrestricted lifestyle was tormented not only by grammatical enclosure, but also by the Enclosure Acts of the nineteenth century, which merchandised land and nature, depriving him of the freedom to wander anonymously through a world common to all.[3]

Culture was being commodified even in Clare's time, as Paulin tells us how the publisher, Drury, simply looked upon Clare's poems as "wares that I have bought, and which will find a market in the great city. I want a broker or a partner to whom I can consign the articles I receive from the manufacturer" (p.50). As Paulin points out (p.xx), Clare's language became "homeless, evicted words powerlessly falling through a social void". Clare offered a fresh, living and alternative way of using language which was being frozen into a homogeneity of written form. Beautiful poetic-sounding words such as – *crizzling* – *sliveth* – *whinneys* – *greening* – *croodling* – *spindling* – *siling* – *struttles* – were, as Paulin asserts (p.53), "crushed under the monolith of Official Standard".

Like James Joyce at a later date, Clare wanted to burst through all types of barriers and enclosures. It is a strange quirk of fate that both he and Joyce's daughter Lucia were to end their days in the same asylum in Northampton. Paulin seems to get to the core of Clare's being when he says (p.52)

> For all the tough, desperate moderation of Clare's professed social opinions in the preasylum years, his potential subconsciousness is a territory of primal hurt and bondage where something wild – some uniquely sensitive spirit – tries to jerk away from all institutions.

Oral poetry, aided by mnemonics, strengthened human memory. Such techniques have all but disappeared now as we lazily consign knowledge to computers.[4] Research is needed to gauge the empirical effects of such loss. Also it must be pointed out, that it is unfair to judge oral poetry with the same critical yardstick that is meant for literary work. The Barthian concept of "death of author" (q.v.) has relevance here, when one considers that *The Iliad* and *The Odyssey* were reputedly written by a collective (cf. Ch 15.1), or that the stories of the mainly illiterate Peig Sayers (1939) were dictated by her for her son to write down. Also, great enriching liberties were taken with many ancient and Biblical stories and poems to suit, what Lehman (1991:165) (in the context of oral-formulaic poetry) calls, "the receptivity of the audience" at different periods and in different cultures. Peig Sayers' retelling of the Resurrection, for example, is set in her own familiar surroundings of the kitchen, and in the context of a cock rising from a boiling cauldron (p.49). And to illustrate cultural differences between East and West, I.A. Richards relates, how in a lecture on Hardy's *Tess of the d'Urbervilles*, which he gave in China, the audience applauded when he concluded with Tess's hanging, because, they believed, she got what she deserved for being unfilial (Berthoff:19).

In a more modern setting, consider the "amputation" we would have suffered if we had not heard the melodious voice of Dylan Thomas reciting his poems, or how impoverished *Under Milkwood* would be in the absence of its wonderful rendition across the airways by his fellow Welshman, Richard Burton. Perhaps there is still hope for the new orality wished for by I.A. Richards, and which has not, as yet, been fully tapped from the potentiality of radio or CD. He believed that such an orality could bring back to us "some of the things we have lost by the intervention of the letter – notably the art of rhetoric and dialectic in the immediacy of a social context" (p. 234).

When Adrienne Rich was in hospital, the poetry coming across the radio enabled her "to engage with states that themselves would deprive us of language and reduce us to passive sufferers" (1993:10). And Mícheál Ó Siadhail (1994:19) cites the case of a troubled lady, who claimed that the effect of listening to his poem being recited on the radio was therapeutic for her, and that it also had the knock-on effect of leading her to attend one of his poetry readings (cf. Ch.15). Thus one could say, that in this context at least, an orality had been established as a continuum.

Does this mean that silent reading is antisocial activity? Not if one discusses what one has read, the discourse being the social product, just as the silently manufactured chair of a carpenter has a social utility in its finished article (Richards, in Berthoff:234). How could such a reader's role be deemed anti-social, when it involves interaction with the work of the artist (cf. Berkeley,

Ch.16), the essence of whose work, according to Frye (1990:55), involves a reaction to the society in which he finds himself. Whether he or she writes in an ivory tower (Yeats), in the street (Baudelaire), in a prison (Behan), on a bus (Lavin), or standing up (Hemingway), has no relevance. What is important is the finished work and how society responds to it. The artist can only make the work; it is the role of society to evaluate it. Additionally, as Denham (Frye:xvii) points out, literature creates visions of what life can be like when freed from the ego, and, consequently, can provide objective and impartial models for social change.

Poetry, therefore, as one of the arts, should be as important as "petrol" (Betjeman) or "vitamin C, communications, laws and hypertension therapy" (Holub). In theory yes, but it must be admitted, that in reality, it only reaches a minority of people.

Besides, as Octavio Paz (1970) indicates, writing has an ambivalent nature. It was originally used by a minority to dominate people, until the use of the printing press by the bourgeoisie broke the monopoly of sacred knowledge. "Writing," according to Paz, "denatures the dialogue between men." The reader is unable to question the writer, or be heard by him, which could account in part for the new emphasis on the reader's role (q.v.) in judging a text.

Three of the activities where speech developed all its powers of rhetoric – poetry, philosophy and politics – over a period of time suffered a sort of mutilation leading to increased passivity among people.[5] Poems should not be hidden away on shelves as mere texts. As already stated, they come alive by the reader's interaction with them.

Part of our problem today is that we are so accustomed to page culture that even at poetry readings and workshops, orality on its own is not considered enough. In many cases it is usual to distribute printed copies of poems to the group before a recitation or reading. Most of us in Western countries have been educated through a literary culture, and we would find it difficult to assess a modern poem merely by hearing it. Perhaps it has something to do with the motionlessness of the written word – something like freezing an action-replay in sport on TV. We frame the poem as we would a painting. Besides, as replays are now part of our modern-day technological expectations, we can always afford not to be alert the first time round.

While mention has already been made of the aesthetic impact of silent visualisation, and the fact that some poems can only be appreciated unvoiced, as in concrete poetry, one wonders what conditions forced us to sacrifice a valued sense. Is it as suggested earlier (Ch. 10:N[2]), that in our sophisticated urban society we have overdeveloped one sense at the expense of others? Is it because, by merely hearing a poem, we are confined to consecutive linearity; or is it due to the bombardment of information technology, which is depriving us of the ability or patience[6] to sit still and hear merely a voice, when there are so many other stimuli, especially visual, competing for our attention. The suggestion that people can be divided into *audiles* and *visiles* has been disproved by psychologists such as the late Paul A. Kolers (1991), who points out that seeing and hearing poems are merely separate engagements, similar to Saussure's *parole* (*voice*) and *langue* (*eye*), which we apply as different strategies to appreciate different types of poetry.

That is not to say that there are not drawbacks with the auditory alone. Tomlinson (1986) posits the idea that sound without sight is an incompleteness

> I heard
> from the farm beyond, a grounded
> churn go down. The sound
> chimed for the wedding of the mind
> with what one could not see.

Sounds can confuse: *murmuring* – *murdering,*[7] *pence* – *pins, hear* – *here* etc., which lead to loss of meaning. Tennyson is said to have become quite irate when a listener failed to recognise the jackdaw which was presented onomatopoeically in one of his poems (Britannica, 2:42). In fact in some languages, such as Classical Irish and Latin, the oral and written forms were in the main mutually unintelligible. Even today in some American Indian cultures such as the Nootka, literary recitations differ from the sounds of ordinary speech (Leech:44). And even in this century, Peig Sayers' (q.v.) oral Irish fluency was of no great assistance in her failure to master the written idiom. Besides, some speakers have better voices than others (cf. Thomas & Burton, q.v.), and apart from pronunciation and enunciation, nuances of meaning may be lost by lack of emphasis, on the one hand, or over-the-top renditions, on the other, although conversely, one could argue, that in a purely silent reading, there can be confusion as regards the poet's tone or mood. Philip Larkin, in a supposed attempt to discourage purchasers of his auditory recording of *Whitsun Weddings*, spoke of the disadvantages of aural poetry

> And when you gain on the sound you lose on the sense: think of all the mishearings, the 'their' and 'there' confusion, the submergence of rhyme, the disappearance of stanza-shape, even the comfort of knowing how far you are from the end (Ricks, 1984:280).

However, as Ricks points out, the effect of such deflation was a great soft sell, and "the rumbling comedy accompanied the order form" (p.280).

11.2 Getting into the Act

What can one say of modern-day performance poetry – the last remnant of oral culture, according to some critics[8], or at its "soggy end," "brain-dead reflexes"? (O'Brien, 1994a). Let us look briefly at some of its history: *Pronunciatio* was one of the five great divisions of Classical rhetoric (the others being *inventio, dispositio, elocutio,* and *memoria*), and it received a renewed impetus in the eighteenth century with the emergence of elocution as an important part of the theory of rhetoric (Princeton:893) (John Clare must have shuddered in his bones at such increasing "correctness" and standardisation). This led to the practice of after-dinner voiced reading in many middle-class Victorian homes, a custom which lasted until the advent of television. However, while a polished and dramatic oral delivery suited some poems, it contrasted sharply with the later conversation styles of poets such as Frost and Auden. In fact, several poets, including Pound and Eliot, deliberately read their work in a monotone, which was intended to subvert such aural expectations.

As regards the "new" oral poetry, it is paradoxical that in the main, it has been distributed not on CD, but rather in traditional book form. There is also the danger in performance poetry that anything will do (cf. O'Brien q.v.). Consider John Whitworth's (1983) comment (albeit smacking of class division) on public house poetry: "I stopped being a working-class culturemonger/Inserting fuck every fourth word" (*Poor Butterflies*). And there may be a danger of reducing the art of poetry by mere performance where, as John Goodby (Dorgan, 1996:134), following on Thomas Kilroy's observation, points out: "a more mature bourgeoisie now cossets the pet artists as hired court jesters".

While performance poetry may be overrated in some cases, nevertheless, in countries such as Hungary it is the only type of poetry that is given acceptability (cf. Ch.12). Here the poet is still the *vates* (*seer*), and as Weissbort (1989:14) informs us, it behoves the poet to point the way to the promised land. Non-performing poets, on the other hand, are treated as second-raters. Perhaps a case could be made for some of the performance verse in the context of jazz poetry, which sprung up in the 40s and 50s in America, the country where jazz itself originated. Many of the "Beat generation" poets (Ginsberg, Kerouac etc.) dabbled in it, and it gained quite a popularity in the late 50s and early 60s, introducing a fresh sense of levity and iconoclasm into poetry (cf. Michael Horovitz's "anglo-saxophone," the equivalent of Orpheus' lyre). It had the effect of revitalising a moribund practice – poetry as recital – and it helped to break down the choking institutionalising effect which theory and the New Criticism had on poetry.

Consider James Simmons on Louis Armstrong: "I ain't got no diploma, said Satchmo/I look into my heart and blow" (*Didn't He Ramble*).

Some of these poems are not only of a very fine quality, but capture the Blues rhythm as well. Adrian Mitchell's (1985) poem about child bullying, *Back in the Playground Blues*, is a good example

> Dreamed I was in a school playground, I was about four feet high
> Yes I dreamed I was back in the playground,
> and standing about four feet high
> The playground was three miles long
> and the playground was five miles wide
>
> It was broken black tarmac with a fence all round
> Broken black dusty tarmac with a high fence running all round
> And it had a special name to it, they called it The Killing Ground.

However, Mitchell is more the exception than the rule as regards the continuance of jazz poetry, because with the foregrounding of pop and rock music in the 60s and later, a decline set in, as many would-be poets picked up the guitar.

Nevertheless, despite its vagaries in fortune, it must be stressed that sound is a vital part of poetry – a part of our "auditory imagination" (Eliot:94). By structuring the nuances of meaning, and even by organising the temporal experience of reading via patterned repetitions, it engages in activities which are fully constitutive of cognition. As Brogan (Princeton:1178-9), puts it: "Language without them is not merely less but *other*. Not to attend to sound in poetry is therefore not to understand poetry at all."

NOTES

[1] Such bias still obtains in the present day. Martin Croghan (1990:29) points out that many theorists "implicitly" treat spoken language as deviant because of their reluctance to refer to it. Contrast such practice with John Mole's (1989:159) suspicion "of any theatre which is not the street", or William Carlos Williams' "no ideas but in things". By referring only to written language, such theorists are limiting their literary range, and as Croghan affirms (p.29), many creative writers – especially of Hiberno-English, which is non-standard – are neglected as a result.

[2] In the *Second Epistle to the Corinthians* (10:9-11), St. Paul states: "So you must not think of me as one who scares you by the letters he writes. 'His letters,' so it is said, 'are weighty and powerful, but when he appears he has no presence, and as a speaker he is beneath contempt'"(New English Bible {1972}, OUP).

[3] Despite Patrick Kavanagh's emphasis on the poverty of the poet in the lines

> Who owns them hungry hills
> that the water-hen and the snipe must have forsaken?
> A poet? Then by heavens he must be poor.
> (*Shancoduff*)

there is also the connotation of the poet as a free wanderer, which links him with Clare's commonage, and as we'll see later, with Pasternak in his conception of his place in the world as that of a "guest of existence". The poet's way of life, in its essence, is the antithesis of the capitalist system, in that he is opposed to the carving up of the world into sections, and the acquisitive claiming of these parts for the purpose of individual profit. The poet's world is free and unfenced. He sees the land as nature, at one with the sea and sky and the air (cf. Ch.7.2). As Kavanagh says, the poet is "king/of banks and stones and every blooming thing" (*Iniskeen Road: July Evening*).

[4] Even in second level State examinations in Ireland, most poems are quoted in full on the English papers, so that the idea of learning by heart is almost a thing of the past; and in some European language examinations, such as Leaving Certificate Spanish, poetry has been removed altogether and replaced by journalistic paragraphs; and in the Junior Certificate in Irish, poetry has been reduced to a mere option (cf. Frye's point {1990:24} from Plato's *Phaedrus*, that Thoth's invention of writing was viewed with suspicion by the ancient Greeks: They believed that writing had more to do with forgetting than remembering, because they felt it would encourage mental laziness).

[5] With the growing importance of intertextual and interdisciplinary studies, however, there is some hope that in the future such ruptures in knowledge can be stitched back together again (cf. Ch.7). Still, the diminution in the number of literary and discursive magazines being published is a matter of continuing concern in this respect (cf. Ch. 15).

[6] Muriel Rukeysen entitled one of her poems: *Reading Time: 1 Minutes 26 Seconds*, which evokes, as Rich (1993:125) points out, "the fast lane of IT, of a world metronomically conditioned, where you time yourself even to read a poem". Must one conclude from this that longer poems and epics are things of the past? As we turn the key that winds the clock, do we also simultaneously "turn a lock/ in the prison of days ..?" (Haines, 1990).

[7] John Crowe Ransome parodied Tennyson's "the murmuring of innumerable bees" as "the murdering of innumerable beeves," to show that even when the overall sound pattern is changed only slightly, the meaning of the words is altered radically, and the "mimetic" effect nearly obliterated (Princeton:1176) (cf. *Ping pong* in Concrete Poetry)

[8] Even this claim could be interpreted as spurious when one considers that, in the main, such poetry is written first before delivery, whereas the real origins of oral poetry lie in ritual.

12 SEEING MESSAGES

12.1 A Spanish Lesson

The problem with ideology in poetry is that its message frequently takes precedence over the merit of the poem (cf. Ch. 13:N[3], where art, *vis-à-vis* religion, has to be contained within the latter's moral gamut or not at all). Just as the religious artist strives firstly for his ideology, so also does the Marxist writer, for whom the aesthetic element always takes second place. The danger for poetry within such parameters is that it could be carried away by AGITPROP, and reduced to mere *prosaismo*, abounding in ordinary language and clichés.

Many protest poets under the Franco regime criticised "poetic" poetry for its fastidious over-refinement" (Wright, 1986:126) (cf. Adorno, q.v.). Blas de Otero, whose aim was to reach "la inmensa mayoría" (Cohen, 1960:444), vitriolically summed up the socialist attitude towards such poets

> Escribo como escupo. Contra el suelo
> (oh esos poetas cursis, con sordina,
> hijos de sus papás) y contra el cielo..
> (*Y el Verso se Hizo Hombre*)

> I write as I spit. Against the ground
> {Oh those genteel poets with a mute,
> daddies' boys} and against the sky.
> (*And the Verse Became Man*)

Poets such as Gabriel Celayo wrote "para transformar el mundo" ("to transform the world"). Language was an instrument to win commitment, and a weapon to deal with the problems of Spain. "La poesía es una arma cargada del futuro" ("poetry is a weapon loaded with the future") (*Cantos íberos*, 1955). Sartre's call for a literature of *engagement* had a great influence on such poets, and Celayo accused non-committed poets of dissipating their energies (cf. Hungary, q.v.), and equated neutrality with opposition. "Ser neutral es pronunciar en contra" ("to be neutral is to declare opposition").

The view held by most of these poets was that the times were not favourable for the pursuit of pure aesthetics. Rafael Alberti, for example, abandoned his earlier surreal work to don the mantle of Marxist ideology. Such action should not be considered strange, when one considers that a conflict of ideologies, such as the Spanish Civil War, also provoked social responses from many non-Spanish intellectuals and writers, such as Hemingway, Spender, Auden and Orwell. Such ideological commitment was seen as a temporary, ethical interruption in their aesthetic pursuits. As Alberti put it in *Coplas de Juan Panadero*

> si no hubiera tantos males
> yo de mis coplas haría
> torres de pavos reales

> If there were not so many evils about
> I would make from my verses
> towers of peacocks.

The problem was what was supposed to have been a temporary ethical interruption, became a lifetime commitment for some poets, as Franco reigned for nearly forty years. While most of the non-Spanish artists, thus temporarily committed, returned to their aesthetic pursuits after the Civil War, it was not to be so for Alberti. He appears to have been caught permanently in the web of such beliefs, and he never really returned to the wonderful poetry (such as *Sobre los Ángeles* {1927}) of his earlier years.

And what of today in a Spain no longer entrapped by ideology or censorship? No longer can poets use excuses to avoid fulfilling their essential role, which is to explore the meaning of existence in an unfettered way. The statement by some intellectuals that "life was better against Franco" is anachronistic, and an indication of a moral identity crisis.[1] However, while the present-day veneration of returned exiles is laudatory, nevertheless the headlong rush to appear ultra-modern can sometimes produce *kitsch*. The coming of democracy does not in itself produce great art; in fact, as Ó Siadhail avers (p.14), freedom can be the hardest challenge of all, and as Silver (1968:68) points out: "There were no geniuses repressed by the dictatorship, and then revealed by the democracy." Being culturally alive does not necessarily mean being artistically alive, and no amount of talk can substitute for the hard grind involved in creative effort.

12.1 *L'art pour l'art*.

But must all social poetry – apart from the "committed" variety – always remain outside the realm of art? Martin Croghan (1988:13) makes the point that judging art on the basis of personal ideology or the morality of the artist is merely interesting as "gossip". Even Yeats refused a request to write a war poem ("I think it better that in times like these/ a poet's mouth be silent"{1990:154}, {which, ironically, contrasts sharply with his outpourings on the happenings in Ireland in 1913 and 1916}). And the normally, personally-taciturn William Shakespeare complained of art being made "tongue-tied by authority" (Moody, 1977:36) (cf. Clare). In present times, Ewa Kuryluk, even more bitterly, decries the politicisation of art. Her words bring to mind Rilke's panther once more: "The world of contemporary politics is a cage. Confined to it, art will mutate to junk. Deprived of art, humans will metamorphose into donkeys" (Becker:18).

Art cannot be fitted into any rule system. Therefore, there is no such thing as politically-correct art; it is a contradiction in terms. One has only to recall the Russian extolment of Gorky, at the expense of Pasternak, to realise the power of publicity and propaganda to turn literary dwarfs into giants, and vice versa.

On the other hand – even if it were a temporary lapse on his part during the revolutionary days of nineteenth century France – Baudelaire decried *l'art pour l'art,* for its lack of "passion which necessarily made it sterile" (Benjamin, 1992:26). We already know Adorno's view on the matter, and Czeslaw Milosz (Alvarez, 1992:12) is quite adamant in his role as witness

> What is poetry which does not save
> Nations or people?
> A connivance with official lies.
> (*Dedication*).

Even Pasternak would find difficulty in disagreeing with such a view, for what he loathed in Stalinism was "the inhuman power of the lie" (*Sunday Times,* 1994), but then his country appears to be almost unique, in that the quality of its poetry rarely suffered for the sake of its message. The suffering was too deep to be otherwise. A poet in Communist Russia was like a Catholic priest in Ireland during the Penal times: both were endangered species; both were venerated by the people; both were preoccupied with symbol; and both sought salvation through language. The analogy could be continued into present times if one compares the huge open-air Mass attendance on a pope's visit to a country, to the tens of thousands listening together in a Russian football stadium to a single poet reciting alone (cf. Arnold q.v.). The respect for the poet in Russia is so great, that books of poetry have been published in editions of as many as 200,000, that sell out within a few days (Todd, 1993:lxxvi).

Part of the reason for such popularity, however, is a much deeper matter than that of the politics of a regime, but is due to the fact that, as Albert Todd points out (p.lxxiv)

> Russian poetry has kept account of people's dreams, hopes, terror, confusion, doubt, anger and moral introspection and has been always fully engaged.

He contrasts such enthusiasm (cf. Rich on Nicaragua, q.v.), with the waning in English poetry, and cites Edmund Wilson, who declared that English poetry has been in decline since the eighteenth century. He also points to the irony in America, where despite the abundance in poetic publication, its audience has diminished, and poets appear to be read now only by other poets (cf. Ch. 17:1).

Where does all this leave ideology? It seems that there is a difference between poetry which is mere AGITPROP and that which has a deep-rooted social concern. Modern Eastern European poets appear to be trying to take a feather out of the Russian cap, in that they are attempting to apply Aristotelian poetic principles to history (i.e., that poetry seeks a higher truth {cf.Ch.13.1}). As Michael March (1990:xvii) points out, when Janos Pilinzsky declared: "The earth betrays me in its embrace, the rest is grace," he replaced history with poetry, which is similar to Frye's call for the removal of "ideological cataracts," so that we can see more of our "mythological conditioning" (p.24).

The responsibility of the artist is to his vision, but if that vision incorporates seeing an injustice in society, then it must be articulated, not for purposes of personal ideology, but in order to illuminate the nature of the injustice itself (without being "colonised" by it, as Marcuse puts it {Becker:114}). For example, e e cummings is justified in his satirical approach to the American extolment of war. In the second part of his poem *next to of course god america* (op. cit.), he uses clichés to turn in upon themselves in mockery of such glorification, and by wrecking patriotic songs and slogans, he reveals "the ultimate degradation of war," as Hawkes points out (p.138), "in the disintegration of language's formal power"

> what could be more beaut
> iful than these heroic dead
> who rushed like lions to the roaring slaughter?

The success of such an approach is all the more noteworthy, if one considers the difficulties for satire in an age of increasing relativism.

The art, therefore, lies, not in the content but in the method, in expressing how – as Anna Akhmatova describes it – "an anxiety collides with a technique" (*Sunday Times*, 1994).

NOTES

[1] Perhaps there is something to be learned from the Spanish experience that can now be applied to post-Communist Russia, as future fears may arise for the well-being of poetry there (despite its present secure position), in the absence of a monolith to strike against. Will poets carry the same respect, now that they are no longer an endangered species? Hopefully. Besides, if we are to reject ideology as a part of art, such a fear should not pose problems. For the artist, it should simply involve a redirection of ontological vision. However, the spectre of materialism is a cause of genuine concern, because, as March points out (p.xviii): "it will replace longing, and poetry will suffer". And with the collapse of Russian communism and the dilution of Western socialism, where can be found the alternative to the increasing global dimension of this seductive and acquisitive power?

13 SEEING THE TURNING WHEELS ADVANCE

13.1 Bombs, Policemen and Plastic Cups

Richard Gregory (1994) relates, how as a child, he saw an elderly policeman weeping by a traffic light. The policeman was weeping because he had helped people across the road all his life and was now being replaced by a machine.

Is all technology good for us? What is its human cost? Must we always accept as progress its latest "mod cons" as they advance in their predictable linearity? One wonders, for example, about the value and ultimate destiny of plastic cups, especially in an ecological context, in our consume-and-throw-away society. And as regards our choked bypasses, who will bypass them? Or perhaps more apocalyptically, what are we to do with our nuclear bombs, and what "just causes" did they support?[1]

Lynn Emanuel (1992) brought the formerly exaggerated and fictitious world and vocabulary of a comic-strip character – Superman – to real and terrifying life in her poem, *The Planet Krypton*. This poem was prompted by watching on TV a nuclear bomb test in the Nevada desert: "the earth falling apart like Superman's planet..." Emanuel creates a surreal image of the bomb as a satanic snake with its "silky hooded, glittering, uncoiling length", as it draws fire up from the well of its own underworld

it hissed and spit, it sizzled like a poker in a toddy.
The bomb was no mind and all body; it sent a fire
of static down the spine. In the dark it glowed like the
coils of an electric stove.

In the wake of nuclear fallout and explosion, where and to whom do we turn? In other words what, if any, are our real resources?[2] With echoes of Yeats ("Things fall apart; the centre cannot hold;/ Mere anarchy is loosed upon the world" {*The Second Coming*, 1990:184}), Adrienne Rich (p.115) describes the scene graphically and poetically, even offering a consolation

> When the landscape buckles and jerks around, when a dust column of debris rises from the collapse of a block of buildings on bodies that could have been your own, when the staves of history fall awry and the barrel of time bursts apart, some turn to prayer, some to poetry: words in the memory, a stained book carried close to the body, the notebook scribbled by hand – a center of gravity.

Perhaps there was something after all (if a little extreme)[3] in Matthew Arnold's prophecy, which he made in that unstable period in 1938: "that most of what now passes with us for religion and philosophy will be replaced by poetry" (p.2). He cites Aristotle's observation that poetry is superior to history in that it possesses a higher truth and a higher seriousness (p.13).[4] In poetry we will find our "consolation and stay" (p.3), because there is not a creed that is not "shaken," or a dogma which is not "questionable," or a received tradition, "which does not threaten to dissolve" (p.1).

13.2 Sight, Sound and Discourse

And what of the putative, benign and benevolent technology, such as telephones and televisions? Can such technology (as we have hinted at earlier) distort our senses? Let us look for a moment at the effects of the telephone on the nature of our discourse. Was it due to the imbalance produced by the phone's overpowering of the aural, its bombarding of other senses, that prompted Peter Ustinov (1991) to exclaim, that when writing, he preferred a bomb to the telephone, "because the bomb you can't answer", and "unless it is a direct hit", it is a preferable "music" by which to write.

The technological insistence of the telephone is captured by Ted Hughes (1983) in his poetic diatribe: *Do Not Pick Up the Telephone*: "That plastic Buddha jars out a Karate Screech." He reminds us how our modern, industrialised world revolves around the telephone, as he warns us: "Do not think the future is yours/it waits upon a telephone."

Despite its sophisticated technology, the telephone's practical application is mainly monologic – it can't be relied upon for twoway communication. It goes into sulks. It shatters expectations: "Your silences are as bad/when you are needed, dumb with the malice of the clairvoyant insane."

Technology seems to be unable to deal holistically with people. It is a false prophet, for, by promising to lead man to greater progress, it is in fact diminishing him by subdividing him atomistically, ironically making him a component of his own creations.

In contrast with the telephone, TV and film, on the other hand, seem to diminish the auditory and other senses for the sake of the visual (cf. Ch.10:N^2). By attempting to make the eye of the camera and that of the spectator one, its minimal effect, at least, is to reduce our critical consciousness. Jean-Louis Baudry goes as far as to claim that it removes individual consciousness altogether (Collins, 1989). Certainly, our "third eye" (that of the mystic) seems to have little or no function in such a medium.

Thus, despite the pervasiveness of its vision, we actually see less through the lens of a camera. So even the well-documented loss of the artistic "aura" to the machine, receives no consolation (cf. Benjamin, 1973:223).[5]

Reality cannot be perceived in its totality (cf. Ortega on perspectivism, q.v.). David Mura, the Japanese-American poet warns of the danger of seeing in only one way. The question he asks (Rich, 1993:121) has particular pertinence here

> What does it mean when poets surrender vast realms of experience to journalists, to political scientists, economists? What does it mean when we allow the "objectivity" of these disciplines to be the sole voice which speaks on events and topics of relevance to us all?

Roland Barthes (1984) reinforces such a doubt, as he adverts to the rhetorical power of the image, and how (with the exception of cinema, which generally follows the art of fiction) it can elude history, and represent a synchronic fact devoid of its original context. As Barthes sees it (p.46), the danger is that

> the more technology develops the diffusion of information (and notably of images), the more it provides the means of masking the constructed meaning under the appearance of the given meaning.

And there is another problem relating to the camera: It is what I call lazy vision, and film itself is not blameless here. Take poets themselves as an example, and see how they are imaged on celluloid. In some contemporary films in which poets have focused – *Dead Poets' Society, Peggy Sue Got Married, Tom and Viv*, they have been presented as stereotypes or caricatures. Film (in Hollywood at least) seems to be unwilling (perhaps influenced by the ethos referred to in Ch.4:N³), or unable to present anything, other than a superficial view of what it means to be a poet.

Despite obstacles, however, some writers, such as the late Dennis Potter, did manage to use TV film creatively and originally. According to Dunkley (Skovmand, 1992:169), Potter used TV as James Joyce used the novel, and van Gogh painting, i.e., "as a multi-layered medium of intense expression". Referring to Potter's almost magically real interior experimentation, Bondebjerg (Skovmand:168) points out that naturalism leads you to believe that you are just a creation of all the imperatives of the world, whereas the non-naturalistic dramatisation of the inside of your head is more likely to remind you of the shreds in your own sovereignty.

The so-called irrational elements in Potter are common to poetry, and his success in combining the popular with the *avant-garde* in his work was proved by the TAM rating. His approach to film needs deeper appraisal.

Perhaps the South American Continent, by means of its "magic realism" in films and literature, could free the Western imagination from its tunnel vision. Or perhaps, too, one should look again at earlier films, even Astaire/Rogers musicals, because they, at least, attempted to maintain a discursive relationship with audiences, where characters looked the camera squarely in the eye.

13.3 A Symphony of Metal

John Haines (1990) speaks of the cramping of modern humanity in "a forest of wires and twisted steel," where nothing thrives "but metal feeding on itself". "War," according to Marinetti, "is beautiful because it initiates the dreamt-of metallisation of the body" (Benjamin, 1973:243). With its grenades and gasmasks and tanks and megaphones and flame throwers and gunfire, as instruments in an orchestra, man can compose a symphony. In his self-alienation he can transform his own destruction into an aesthetic pleasure.

As Benjamin points out (p.244), there is a huge discrepancy "between the tremendous means of production and their inadequate utilisation in the process of production". In other words, instead of using technology to tackle problems such as unemployment, or as Benjamin puts it: "to drop seeds from airplanes", it prefers to drop incendiary bombs.

Such "dystopic landscapes," as Lash (Turner, 1990:73) describes them in a Baudrillardian context, are reflected in some postmodern films such as *Blade Runner* (1982), which represents a world in physical and psychological decay (but brilliantly done – hence the aesthetic element). It is interesting to contrast the expense ($27 million) and depth of research that went into "authenticating" what was essentially a science fiction movie, and the poor showing in relation to the poet-films mentioned earlier.

13.4 Two Views of Brooklyn Bridge

How can poets see through steel? Not all poets shared Eliot's pessimism, or viewed the modern world as a "waste land". In his poem *Brooklyn Bridge*, the Russian poet, Vladimir Majakovskij (1925) admired "the miles of steel" in the bridge, because

> upon it my vision comes to life, erect –
> here's a fight for construction instead of style,
> an austere disposition of bolts and steel.

Hart Crane was even more bewitched than Majakovskij by this bridge. Basically a late romantic, he was influenced by Walt Whitman, but sought to find an equivalent of Whitman's sublime rural wilderness in a modern, urban technological context.

While T.S. Eliot also held sway over him, Crane rejected his mentor's pessimism about the modern age, particularly as portrayed in the *Waste Land* (1922). Crane wanted to affirm the machine age, by means of a transformation of vision, which involved attempting to heighten ordinary life through ecstatic expression. This he tried to do in his epic poem *The Bridge* (1930).

For Crane, Brooklyn Bridge represents something more than merely a man-made construction. He marvels at its wires of steel, seeing them, not as Haines (q.v.) does – as twisted symbols of humanity, but rather as strings with which to create music: "How could mere toil align thy choiring strings!" (cf. Marinetti's symphony, q.v.).

The sheer size and power of the bridge enable it to touch the heavens, where it is privy to "the immaculate sigh of stars", and whence it can "condense eternity". And with its great strength and illumination "we have seen night lifted in thine arms". The bridge is a colossus, a god that bestrides "the prairies dreaming sod" (cf. Whitman, q.v.).

Majakovskij and Crane, however, are not simply condoning or extolling technology. They know the advancing wheels cannot be turned back. They have chosen to revolve with them, not fatalistically, but in an attempt, by so doing, to gain further insights into what makes the world go round.

Perhaps, too, such an approach is more meaningful than that of the increasing number of people who use technology to cocoon themselves emotionally from the real world, where they can exclaim defiantly through the lips of Bertold Brecht (speaking about storms): "all they touch now is our aerials" (*Concerning Spring*, 1987).

NOTES

[1] Apart from the well-documented destructiveness of nuclear bombs (Hiroshima, Nagasaki), even a supposed knowledge of their technology proved lethal for a young American couple, the Rosenbergs, parents of two young children at the time. In 1953 they were put to death by electric chair, accused of passing the secret of the atom bomb to the Soviet Union. Evidence today overwhelmingly suggests that these people were innocent, and were treated as hapless scapegoats in Cold-War hysteria (Miller, 1994:38-44).

[2] It is a perverted twist of logic that when the first atom bomb was exploded in Los Alamos in 1945, the director of the project, Robert Oppenheimer, a professed pacifist and believer in Sanskrit, had recourse to poetry to sum up his emotion. He quoted from the Hindu epic poem, the *Bhavagad Gita*: "I am become Death, the destroyer of worlds" (Millar, 1994:30).

[3] Before considering poetry and religion in the context of mutual exclusion, it is worth bearing in mind that there is a frequent overlap between the two (and indeed with philosophy also). Vico informs us that poetry actually arose out of divination (Bloom, 1976:3). Many poets (Milton, Dante, Donne, Pasternak, Hopkins etc.) have dealt with religion in their poetry, and the reverse is also true, i.e., scriptural writers have had recourse to poetry. Much of the beauty of Biblical poetry has a vernacular (q.v.) base: "I am the rose of Sharon and the lily of the valleys" (*The Song of Solomon*). *The Book of Psalms* and *The Song of David* are universally acclaimed as great poetry, and *The Beatitudes* is a parallelist's (q.v.) delight.

However, religion does not consciously ally itself to either science or art. As Sapir (1949:123) points out, it seeks neither the "objective enlightenment" of science, nor "the strange equilibrium, the sensuous harmony, of aesthetic experience." The problem religion has *vis-à-vis* art, is that it limits art within its moral confines, so that in time of crisis art and religion tend to go their separate ways (cf. Hopkins' temporary abandonment of poetry as a form of asceticism {Bullock, 1983:339}.Nevertheless, it is also interesting to reflect that when Hopkins' crisis revolved around his own personal beliefs (as distinct from a more objective world concern), he could not escape poetry, and actually produced his finest work at that time (*The Terrible Sonnets*).

Perhaps if Arnold had used the word spirituality instead of religion in his prophecy, he would have been nearer the mark. There is undoubtedly a spiritual crisis in the Western world, and Christian myths and symbols are losing their power (are "fossilised," according to Jung). The age cries out for spirit, and art is the witness to that need (cf. note[4]).

[4] Such an observation tallies with Heidegger's idea of the function of art as "the setting-into-work of truth" (Vattimo, 1988:60). Also I.A. Richards (1926:82-3), decrying science for its failure to satisfy emotionally and seeing literature as a way of reconstructing social order, also lends support to Arnold, when he states: "Poetry is capable of saving us; it is a perfectly possible means of overcoming chaos. And Vattimo (p.67), scanning the work of Bloch, Adorno and Marcuse, reinvigorates such beliefs for the modern era

> A work of art can be seen as a truly prophetic and utopian figuration of an alternative world or of a harmonised existence with regard to which the existing order is revealed in its injustice and inauthenticity.

[5] ... "that which withers in the age of mechanical reproduction is the aura of the work of art... By making many reproductions it (the machine) substitutes a plurality of copies for a unique existence" (Benjamin, 1973:223). Don DeLillo illustrates Benjamin's prophetic ideas in *Libra* (1989), where he adverts to the irony of sophisticated technology being used merely for the purpose of endless and inane repetition. He cites the infinitely repeated rerunning of the televised assassination of J.F. Kennedy, where the president is shot and reshot again and again, multiplied

like a Warhol Coca Cola can, or multi-images of Marilyn Monroe. History is turned into pastiche, but most frightening, is the dulling of all feelings of outrage

> After some hours the horror became mechanical. They kept racking films, running shadows through the machine. It was a process that drained life from the men in the picture, sealed them in the frame (p.447).

Or consider how at the end of *Mao II* (1992), in Beirut − where human exhaustion is palpable − the insatiable, ubiquitous camera must take yet another shot, and thus "the dead city is photographed one more time" (p.241).

14 SEEING ICE FOR THE FIRST TIME

In *Cien Años de Soledad* by Gabriel García Márquez (1967), when Aureliano is taken by his father to see ice for the first time, something ordinary is presented as if it were extraordinary, by describing the phenomenon through the eyes of the boy.

Poetry acts in a similar way, illuminating with new language the ordinary, mundane and the quotidian. As Hawkes puts it (p.62), its function is "to counteract the process of habituation encouraged by routine everyday modes of perception". It sees a world in a "grain of sand" (Blake, in Hayward, 1956:243), or expresses wonder at "a stick carried down a stream," or "wherever life pours ordinary plenty" (Kavanagh, 1984). It enables us to see the pristine in the defiled, as Blake asserts: "Every harlot was a virgin once" (p.248). It makes us look again more deeply at things and people, to get behind the hidden, the obfuscating, the obscure in order to extricate the real.

It slices through guile and hypocrisy warning us, as in Blake, of the "look of soft deceit," and how our senses can be fooled in a dishonest world. "Why cannot the ear be closed to its own destruction/Or the glistening eye to the poison of a smile?" (from *The Book of Thel* {Hayward:246}).

In a modern setting, one wonders if Christmas will ever be the same again after Seamus Heaney's (1966) observation of the stuffed turkey as "a skin bag plumped with inky putty", although Holub's (1990) gory details of the killing of the Christmas carp are more chilling than any horror movie, as he turns the smug season of good will on its head singing

> "These are my happiest days; these are my golden days,"
> or
> "The starry above me and the moral law within me,"
> or
> "And yet it moves,"
> or at least
> "Hallelujah!"

The choice element is highly satirical here reminding one of the choice of hymns that may be sung in church on festive occasions for the delectation of all. It is reminiscent of cummings' parody of some American sacred cows, as he muffles and overwhelms the inherited traditional social forms with the mouthings of politicians: "by gorry/by jingo by gee by gosh by gum" (Hawkes:138).

Or consider two poets (Holub and Kennelly) on football: "something... rolls near the rheumatic post/someone kicks it and "the unrinsed mouths of thousands open wide/in a stifling explosion of silence/like trilobites yelling Goal (Holub: *On the Origin of Football*). Kennelly (1991:166), in *The Madness of Football*, blends history and poetry when he records how the RIC were instructed to open fire on the crowds in Croke Park, something which explains the various puns in the poem: "Was there a Final feeling that Sunday... A breakthrough in virile craft and art?/The papers forecast a battle royal... I'm shot through with the madness of football./ Run, hit, kick, score, win. Win. That's all."

Or consider how Kavanagh's dilapidated garden (Harmon, 1981:77) can be transformed by poetry acting through the imagination of a child-poet

> In the thistly hedge old boots were flying sandals
> By which we travelled through the childhood skies,
> Old buckets rusty-holed with half-hung handles
> Were drums to play when old men married wives.

Or do we shudder at Larkin's assertion (1988:121) of creeping age, in mothers' fading beauty "pushing them to the side of their own lives" (*Afternoons*)?

Or Michael Davitt's warning (Fallon, 1990:340) of the wasteful years and false haven afforded by drink?

> Trí bliana is dhá scór ag déanamh
> A bhuilín i bparthas cleasach an tí óil
> (*Ciorrú Bóthair*)

> Reaching forty-three
> Loafing in the deluded paradise of the pub.
> (*Shortening the Road*. Trans. Philip Casey)

Or on a lighter note in Brendan Kennelly (p.257), as he pokes fun at high moral stances, by describing a male "turn-on" provoked by the contemplation of a nude mannequin in Brown Thomas' window in Dublin's Grafton Street.

Or as we go about our domestic chores, in the "great indoors" with Craig Raine (1978), will vacuum cleaning be like filling a cow's bladder?

> The vacuum cleaner grazes
> over the carpet, lowing
> its udder a swollen wobble...
> (*An Enquiry into Two Inches of Ivory*)

And as night falls, he "watches light ripen the electric pear".

Or what could be more ordinary than the nose?[1] Peter Redgrave (1994:128), tries to get to the origin of its meaning (cf. stanza, q.v.)

> Nostril:
> Once spelt 'nosethrill'
> A double quiver packed with nasal arrows,
> Those hairy old foresters.
> (*The Olfactors*)

However, the anguish of life is no stranger to poetry, and Katie Donovan (1993) in *Pattern* makes one realise that cyclical pain can never be taken for granted

> Pain arrives,
> on the slightest pretext,
> making her home
> in my belly —
> a *monthly* visit is not enough.

Even the word pain itself, according to Holub, does not describe the experience of pain but actually replaces it. It is a form of silencing. Such a view is interesting in a medical context, when one considers how some patients are treated. Eliot's (1953:30) comment that the purpose of poetry is not to wallow in emotion, but to "escape" it, expresses a similar idea, i.e., by articulating the hurt, it will somehow disappear.

Eavan Boland (1994) describes the passing of summer as "a place mislaid between expectation and memory" (*Moths*), and the loss of love's intensity is illustrated in the detail of the lover who once stood "with snow on the shoulder of your coat", but words are now "shadows" that can no longer be made tangible by the lover (*Love*).

On childbirth, she becomes the universal mother, finding consolation in knowing that "the world is less bitter to me/because you will re-tell the story".

Craig Raine (1994) in *History: The Home Movie*, combines poetry and novel in filmic form (i.e., in the visual brevity of the takes) and captures the rich pristine quality of the ordinary: a baby's mouth "pulls like a plug hole"; a Steinway piano "grins like a finned shark"; hydrangeas appear in "subtle shades of litmus"; noses peel in August "like jersey potatoes". Raine sees the world with the freshness of a creature from outer space (cf. his second volume of poems *A Martian Sends a Postcard Home* {1979}). His vision is a type of eidetic retrieval of domestic things, often not expressed in poetry. For him, "art is noticing the thing at the edge of your vision that doesn't quite fit" (Cornwell, 1994:39). What Paulin (1992:109), says of Emily Dickinson could equally apply here: "She inflates the quotidian with such momentousness that it almost bursts in the writing."

The venom with which we treat each other as human beings is not ignored by modern poets. Holub calls on surgical knowledge to abet his poetry when he exclaims: "We write upon each other with scalpels" (*On the Origin of 6PM*). Kennelly's *City of Knockers*, captures a similar theme

> Let us now praise the city of knockers
> In the streets of sneer and the pubs of mock;
> These are the artists, my vicious brothers
> whose dreams have come unstuck.

There is humour in Holub, as in *Brief Reflection on Eyes*, he renews the mock heroic: "Goddesses, gods, fear and Twiggy have very large eyes." However, he sends a chill down our spines in his *Brief Reflection on Test Tubes*, which starts as an apparent attack on the cruelty of scientific experiments, but, as we approach the end of the poem, we realise that the test tube is a metaphor for the world, and we humans are the experiment

> That's the real joke
> which makes you forget for a while
> that really you yourself are
>
> In the test-tube.

(cf. Rilke's cage, or Wittgenstein's bottle). Or consider the way he looks at words in his *Brief Reflection on the Flood*

> A real flood means that balloon-bubbles
> come from our mouths
> and we think they are
> words.

The Flood, because it is remote and Biblical, needs to be looked at anew. The subaqueous denotation would seem to suggest that in our modern information society, we are being drowned in a sea of words, but there is also the connotation of bubbles used to enclose speech in cartoon and comic strips? Beneath our suave exterior, is "progress" turning us into clowns? Under his microscope, Holub deflates the grandiose, the lyrical[2] and brings us down to earth, to view the thing of the here-and-now, what it carries inside it, and how it relates to other things

> All that is left
> is a cup of tea
> the deepest ocean in the world.
> (*Harbour*)

Thus, by means of the imagination, the artist is able to render the ordinary experiences of everyday life in terms of acts and objects, dissociated from their practical consequences, so that as Gunn (1987:104) puts it: "We can perceive their potential as opposed to their actual meaning." And it is this potentialising, this subjunctivising of the world, always seeing alternatives, that is a fundamental component of artistic engagement.

NOTES

[1] The sense of smell may not appear as dominant in art as some of the other senses, but it should not be neglected, particularly in its role as provoker of memory. Proust proved its inspirational power in this regard, and many poets try to encapsulate the olfactory into their work (cf. Heaney's "I loved the dark drop, the trapped sky, the smells/Of waterweed, fungus and dank moss" {*Personal Helicon*, 1966:57}).

[2] Holub justified his professed anti-lyricism because he had to write for many years under a Communist regime in Czechoslovakia. However, sometimes he surprises us and perhaps himself − a Freudian slip? − by allowing the lyrical to creep into his lines

> There is no mystery
> except the thread which from our hands
> leads us round the far side of things
> round the collar of the landscape
> and up the sleeve of a star.
> (*The Root of the Matter*)

Apart from the lyricism of the "star", it is interesting to note how similar his attempt to view the world by getting "round the far side of things" is to that of Craig Raine's "noticing the thing at the end of your vision" (q.v.).

15 VISION IN THE MARKET PLACE

15.1 A Poetic Society

According to Giambattista Vico (q.v.), the eighteenth century anti-Cartesian author of *Scienza Nuova* (1725), the first language used by primitive people was full of passion, imagination and myth, and was therefore poetic. Such was the imaginative power of these early ancestors, that they were able to create a world of "magic personification, of living deities expressing their might and their will by the natural phenomena (Auerbach, 1959:191).

However, although this society was poetic, it was, according to Vico, "a severe poem", being rigidly patriarchal, and conservative. No opposition or innovation could be tolerated, because all knowledge to these people was of divine or mystical origin. They created powerful metaphors to express a world, which was not rational, but enchanted and fantastic. Everyone was a poet by his very nature. As Auerbach points out (p.192), "their wisdom, their metaphysics, their laws, all their life was 'poetic'".

With this realisation, that all our first ancestors were poets, Vico was thus enabled to initiate the theory that Homer was not an individual poet (q.v.), but a poetical myth, a product of folk genius, which led, over long periods of time to the creation of epics.

Eventually, however, the secrecy and inviolability of such a people were threatened, when the slaves (former nomads), whom they kept, rebelled, and usurped from the heroes, their rights and privileges. Thus, over a period of time, an imaginative and poetic way of life (aristocratic in a sense {cf. Yeats' longing for such a society}) – "the age of the gods" – ceded its rich, creative power to rationalism, and "the age of men". Poetry was thus reduced, from being intrinsic to life, to what Auerbach calls (p.193): "a mere embellishment" of it, "an elegant pastime" (cf. Rich's "garnish).

However, for Vico, the imaginative and metaphorical power of these primitive people, their ability to see a world poetically, cyclically, and with a strict harmony, that pervaded all their life, made them a model of creative greatness.

15.2 The Unmoored Boat

When orality gave way to literacy, what had been a communal, closely-knit form of poetic calling, surrendered to one that was individual, selective and distant. Such a landscape was not totally bleak in that the modern poet, by breaking from the binding and conservative nature of the tribe[1]. was able to experiment and innovate, albeit in an alienated way. Instead of being a conveyor of old and unified truths, the poet was now free to embark on new discoveries, but not without being shipwrecked from time to time on the sharp rocks of censorship (q.v.).

When Arthur Symons declared that "the poet has no more part in society than the monk in domestic life" (McLeish, 1960:112), he was missing a vital point: it is society which assigns poets to their roles, important or not, and thus the very act of ignoring poetry is itself a social issue.

However, it wasn't simply due to the switch from an oral to a written culture which alienated the poet – although that played its part, leading as it did, to what

Eliot called: "a dissociation of sensibility" (p.117). There were deeper reasons, caused by changes that occurred in society itself.

Accounts of the fragmentation (almost a cliché now) of society – communally, discursively and ethically – after two world wars, are well documented. Many modern cities have now become diseased, with Aids as their metaphor; suicide manuals have become best sellers, and any sense of stability has broken down in a world overhung by a nuclear threat. Robert Lowell (Heaney, 1988:146) captures such a mood

> All autumn, the chafe and jar
> of nuclear war;
> we have talked our extinction to death.
> I swim like a minnow
> behind my studio window.
> (*Fall 1961*)

The earth has become a "hospital," said Larkin. Then poetry is its "medicine", retorted Hughes, describing it as the "psychological component of the immune system" (Wilmer, 1995), perhaps with Emily Dickinson in mind: "He ate and drank the precious Words/His spirit grew robust" (Rich, 1993:103).

Such fragmentation, or rather mutilation, was caught in the photographic sequence *Dolls* by Hans Bellmer (1936), where mannequins were cut up into sections and displayed in their dismembered parts. These photographs influenced Freud. Lacan, and later Dalí (cf. the latter's fetishisation of the fragmentation of the body in *The Phenomenon of Ecstasy*).

Mutilation is also a motif which runs through the work of the contemporary French novelist, Michel Tournier (cf. Whitman's subversive use of the body, q.v.). Emma Wilson (1993) traced another influence in this writer's work, something which is equally relevant for modern society: that of Plato's *Symposium*, where Zeus divides man in two, to make him weaker, and so that he will seek salvation. Thus man is not complete in the world (his potentialities exceed their realisability, as Heller points out {Gunn:115}); he only possesses half of himself, and his purpose in life is to seek his twin, his other half. Such fulfilment can be achieved through art (cf. *suture*, q.v.). But in a world that is broken, it can only be done by a very lonely voyaging.

15.3 The Broken Chain

When P.D. Roberts (1986:141) considers the role of the poet in society, he conjures up an image of a crowded marketplace, where vendors, musicians, painters, and acrobats all intermingle. Then in their midst

> we find someone who is doing nothing more than playing with words –
> the words of our language, but sounding different somehow. Their flow
> sets up a strong rhythmic awareness in the minds of all who hear them.
> Although we may not understand all the meaning of the words, we are
> attracted by the sound they make, and what they suggest. But some stay
> only for a moment or two, and then pass on to other attractions.

To many people poetry is only a game, and there are other more tangible things with which to divert themselves.

Children have always responded to puns, riddles, games. Even Ó Siadhail (p.7) mentions his first incipient taste for poetry in the rhyming jingle of skipping games.

But what goes wrong as we carry on into adulthood? Where does the chain lose its link? Why is the child's uninhibited sense of verbal wonder not carried forward into what Roberts (p.145) calls "the most complex and 'adult' word-game of all: the poem?" We have already mentioned the Western societal bias towards poetry

(cf. Yeats' "apples" q.v.). But why is this so? Why does poetry remain external to most peoples' experience? Is the "Killing Ground", referred to earlier, also an imaginative moratorium? Has it to do with examinations? It cannot simply be a matter of poetry being badly taught (schools can only reflect, but cannot create society's mores, and besides, there are many fine teachers). Perhaps it would be more beneficial to examine, not why poetry may be badly taught, but why it is not taught at all in some instances (cf. Ch.11:N[4]).

People are sometimes embarrassed by poetry, and a sophisticated age, such as ours, does not condone embarrassment lightly. A contemplative approach to life in our fast lane is now deemed anti-social behaviour.[2] Even Wordsworth, in his latter years, was lampooned by *Punch* for taking dictation from illiterate peasants.

Seriousness itself is "up for grabs," as Sontag points out (Becker:128), and it is not meant in the sense of humourlessness – there are many examples of humour in poetry, some of which we have already seen. But humour can be a bully, and a loud guffaw can be a great silencer, muffling creative thought into "safe" havens of superficiality (cf. outsiderhood, q.v.).

And yet the poetic need won't go away. Witness the huge number of surreptitious and often pseudonymous entries to myriad poetry competitions, or consider the consistency in the sale of poetry anthologies for private ingestion (Seamus Heaney's sales equal that of any best-selling novelist).

So where lies the poet's role in society? Too much entrapment, on what Denham (Frye:xvii) calls "the treadmill of history" makes art become parasitic on something else (as we have seen with protest poetry). On the other hand, too much aloofness, can, as Rich (1993:231) says, make the art

> become rarefied, self-reflecting, complicit with the circumstances of its making, cut off from a larger, richer and more disturbing life.

It seems, therefore, that the poet's role lies somewhere in between, i.e., in a constant dialectic between engagement and detachment.

15.4 A Busy Day at the Office

Let us glance at how one modern, professional poet, Mícheál Ó Siadhail, perceived his role: He worked on an arts council (1988-93), so a lot of his time was taken up with committees. This is interesting in itself, because few poets (Heaney excepted, {but then, even he is an academic}), unlike many novelists, are self-supportive from their art alone, and in fact most are actually teachers or lecturers. Widening his work on committees into a metaphorical sense, Ó Siadhail (1994:11) saw his role as that of a secretary of society's secrets "in the rush of our living...minuting our shifting perceptions of ourselves."

His "socialisation" is by way of poetry readings in public and through the media (cf. his radio-broadcast impact on the troubled lady, q.v.). He would feel his role fulfilled, he says, rather humbly, if his words could "move just a little, someone's flagging heart" (p.8). The poet, ironically, can break down isolation in others through words proceeding from his own isolation.

Unfortunately, because of the general anonymity of poetry consumption today, the profundity of such an effect is difficult to gauge, and besides, as Ó Siadhail (p.18) asks: "Who has any command over the complete otherness of response?" However, one could certainly add, that poetry can break through class barriers. An example of this is how a relationship developed, through poetry, between the War poets, Wilfred Owen and his superior officer, Siegfried Sassoon, despite the class-ridden nature of English society.

Ó Siadhail, like all good poets, also sees his role as one who recharges language, as one who engages in *reverdissement*, which is in keeping with his view of poetry as part of an ecosystem, where words are exploited and polluted for purposes of consumerism.

15.5 How Fares the Business?

Has poetry progressed in the marketplace since the time of Joyce's *Pomes Penyeach* (1927), or since Kavanagh peddled his literary wares on broadsheets in the 50s and 60s? The tradition of selling poems on the streets is continued today by poets such as Pat Ingoldsby, and poetic extracts can even be read on trains now (the Dublin Dart), which makes a pleasant change from the ubiquitous consumer-advertising. There have been even poetry request programmes on the radio (*Along the Backwater*). In the Irish government one of our previous ministers (Michael D. Higgins) is himself a poet; and our president, like the previous one, genuinely takes poets under her wing, and shows, as she peppers her speeches with their words, that she is not afraid to take counsel from them.[3]

However, there is a worrying trend: the decline in the *little magazine*. This is ironic when one considers that newsagents are stretched, with a widening range of glossies, to cater for just about every pursuit other than poetry. The fragmentation of discourse in our era (cf. Ch.11:N[5]) seems to be reflected, in the paucity of what were formerly wide-ranging, literary and intellectual papers (*Hibernia, Stet* etc.).[4] And some of those which remain in journal form are removed from the marketplace, and hidden in elitist or academic cloisters. Perhaps the electronic media have done some damage here (cf. Richards' dream of a new orality, q.v.), and such a state of affairs represents a yawning gap in modern-day communication. If, as Mandelstram says, we measure a civilisation by the number of its poetry readers, and if we take that term in its broad spiritual sense, one wonders what kind of society we are producing for the future.

NOTES

[1] The conservative power of the tribe was not of a puritan nature (cf. vernacular poetry), but more in the literal meaning of the word: the keeping or saving of divinely handed-down myths and customs, which were anything but sexually restrained, but which nevertheless could not be contravened.

[2] Walter Benjamin (1973:240) points out, that the former intensity of concentration applied before works of art – paralleled for example, by a monk in a cell beholding a statue – has been removed from our lives by kinetics (cf. Salinas).

[3] Cf. Shelley's view of poets as "the unacknowledged legislators of the world" (*Defense of Poetry*). Dawson (1980) points out that poets can exert influence over opinion, as the world must firstly be transformed in imagination before it can be changed politically. And Heaney (1988:92) subtly indicates that because poetry is its own vindicating force, it therefore has been granted the right to govern, and "we as readers submit to its jurisdiction of achieved form". Heaney has in mind here, not so much an ethical right, as a biological right (cf. Ch.2) where the poet, in the words of Anna Swir, whom he cites (p.93), "becomes an antenna, capturing the voices of the world".

[4] Additionally, within the Irish context, the much loved *Krino* and *The Honest Ulsterman* folded in 1996 and 2003 respectively. Still, there are stalwarts such as *Poetry Ireland Review, Cyphers, Irish Pages, The Dublin Review* and more recently with a ray of hope for the twenty first century, *The Stinging Fly* magazine with its publishing press, and *Cúirt Review, Crannóg, West 47, The Black Mountain Review, Southword, Cork Literary Review, The Shop,* and *Windows Publications.*

16 SEEING DOUBLE

16.1 A Dual Heritage

W. B. Yeats monopolised so many Irish myths that his successors were left
wondering, where to now? He tried to resist the "filthy modern tide". But tides are
phenomena we cannot stop, which perhaps makes James Joyce (who opened the
floodgates) the real poetic precursor to new generations rather than Yeats. It could
be argued that Yeats, because of his immersion in Irish myths and high ideals, did
not address the real world, the world of the ordinary, of the matter of fact. New
myths were found in the quotidian. As already alluded to (Chap.14), Patrick
Kavanagh was one of the artists who could find poetry in a stick floating down a
stream. Michael Hartnett (1975), in a culinary metaphor gets to the crux of the
matter

> Chef Yeats, that master of the use of herbs
> could raise mere stew to a glorious height,
> pinch of saga, soupçon of philosophy
> carefully stirred in to get the flavour right,
> and cook a poem around the basic verbs.
> Our commis-chefs attend and learn the trade,
> bemoan the scraps of Gaelic that they know:
> add to a simple Anglo-Saxon stock
> Cúchulainn's marrow-bones to marinate,
> a dash of Ó Rathaille simmered slow,

a glass of University hic-haec-hoc:
sniff and stand back and proudly offer you
the celebrated Anglo-Irish stew.
(from *A Farewell to English*)

But apart from the polarity of myth making and the pursuit of the ordinary, what other dualities exist in an Irish context? Dennis Donoghue (1987), citing division as the predominant characteristic of Ireland, lists examples

> Catholic and Protestant, Nationalist and Unionist, Ireland and England, North and South, the country and the one bloated city of Dublin, Gaelic Ireland and Anglo-Ireland, the comfortable and the poor. Farmers and P.A.Y.E. workers, pro-Treaty and anti-Treaty, child and parents, the Irish and the English languages, the visible Ireland and the hidden Ireland, landlord and tenant, the Big House and the hovel. To which it is now necessary to add: a defensive church and an increasingly secular state, Irish law and European law.

When a language dies, the dead voices, as Máirtín Ó Cadhain (1949) tells us, "make a noise like wings". This resonance is later reiterated by Eavan Boland (2001) in *Irish Poetry*, her tribute to Michael Hartnett, as she wondered "how the sound of a bird's wing in a lost language sounded". What the Irish poet inherits is a dual culture of Gaelic and English, and translating from one to the other is, as Michael Cronin (1996:181) points out, among other things, "an act of self-understanding". With their different grammars it is like having two world views (cf. Sapir/Whorf, q.v.) which poets such as Thomas Kinsella and Austin Clarke, who recognised Gaelic as the oldest vernacular literature in Western Europe, found an enriching experience as they incorporated Ireland's past, whether historical (Kinsella) or metrical (Clarke), into their contemporary work. Entangled words from the Gaelic constantly insinuate themselves into English as spoken and written in Ireland. Paul Durcan (1980) for example, mocks more than that tendency in the title of his poem *The Boy Who Was Conceived in the Leithreas (lavatory)*.

The two world views presented by the two cultures and languages are not always felicitously complementary. This is illustrated by Brendan Behan's Gaelic play, *An Giall*, a sensitive love story and study of Anglo-Irish relations which, as Declan Kiberd (1991:520) points out, becomes reduced, when translated into the English for the London stage as *The Hostage,* to a raucous stage-Irish romp with fashionable references to the Profumo scandal and the starlet Jane Mansfield.

The reverse of course can take place, too, where Michael Hartnett (1987) translates from his own Irish imaginatively into English. Lines on *The Hare* from *A Necklace of Wrens* read

> Maith dom é, a chailín
> Ní raibh aon scian agam
> Chun do chlann a shábháil
> Maith dom é

> Forgive me, girl
> I had no knife
> To cut your children free
> Forgive me

The literal translation of the third line is "to save your family". Hartnett prefers to translate it as "to cut your children free". This, as Eugene O'Brien (McDonagh, 2006:153) tells us, is Hartnett, the dual-language poet, creating a different meaning across the page, and across linguistic systems. Or as Terence Brown (*Krino*, 1996: 137) puts it

> The poet seeks for alternative linguistic perspectives from which to survey the landscape. Irish offers one such perspective, that angle that may permit innovatory perception, radical envisioning.

The caveat, however, as regards the older culture, was not to hark back to it as a prelapsarian state, and above all not to wallow in it (cf. Eliot, q.v.). Gerald Dawe (1995:32) quotes Flannery O'Connor from her speech "on the gifts of the region"

...you (may) have seen these gifts abused so often that you have become self-conscious about using them. There is nothing worse than the writer who doesn't use the gifts of the region, but wallows in them.

Hartnett (2001) in *Sibelius in Silence* weeps but doesn't wallow: "They say my music weeps for the days/when my people ate the bark from trees."

Eavan Boland (1994) in *Lava Cameo* continues the warning

> there is a way of making free with the past,
> a pastiche of what is
> real and what is
> not, which can only be
> justified if you think of it
>
> not as sculpture but syntax.

The past on the other hand is very real for John Montague (1961); it is even discernible in the title of one of his poems, *Like Dolmens Round My Childhood The Old People*. The poet explains

> I was harnessing an artesian energy from many silent centuries. These hushed, orphaned voices whispered partly in another language, emphasising the ironies of my own name: Tadhg or Tague transformed into the more stylish Montague (*The Poets Chair*:14-15)[1].

For Thomas Kinsella (1996) the past was a "tight beat tapping out endless calls into the dark" (*Baggot Street Deserta*).

For Seamus Heaney (1975) the process involves archaeological digging through bogland and in the city going deeply down through palimpsests to Viking Dublin

> My words lick around
> cobbled quays, go hunting
> lightly as pampooties
> over the skull-capped ground

And as he follows into the mud he invokes the ancestors

Old father, be with us.
Old cunning assessors
of feuds and of sites
for ambush or town.
(*Viking Dublin: Trial Pieces*)

But to do this digging and express the findings in the English language was not without its teething problems as Connemara-born Mary O'Malley (1993), echoing Joyce, avers, as she tried to come to terms with Received English

It was hard and slippery as pebbles
full of cornered consonants
and pinched vowels, all said
from the front of the mouth
no softness, so sorrow, no sweet lullabies
until we took it by the neck and shook it.

What was lost through the years of colonial conquest, Kinsella in verse translations tries to recapture in Seán Ó Tuama's *An Duanaire, poems of the dispossessed, an anthology of Gaelic poetry spanning three hundred years from 1600-1900.* The anthology, a parallel text, is according to Seamus Heaney (1988:31) "educative, historically sensitive and designed to be representative of a whole Irish continuum in which public events and private ways of feeling have nourished each other".

It must also be pointed out that, equally, a reverse insight applied towards nineteen thirties Ireland in the poetry of Louis MacNeice (q.v.), the Belfast-born son of a Church of Ireland rector. Living away from the country equipped the poet with the vision of outsiderhood (q.v.) and thus, "banned for ever from the candle of the Irish poor" (*Carrigfergus*, 1937), he explored and attacked not so much an Ireland as a victim of empire, but rather as a victim of its own shallowness, of Puritanism ("Let the censor be busy on the books") and of hypocrisy which

... gives her children neither sense nor money
Who slouch around the world with a gesture and a brogue
And a faggot of useless memories.

Topography – the ghosts of place – *or dinnseanchas,* has seeped from the Gaelic into Irish poetry evidenced by the frequency in which place names are invoked in various poems by Kavanagh, Heaney and Hartnett as well as in Richard Murphy's *The Battle of Aughrim* and John Montague's *The Rough Field.* The place names, sacred in the Gaelic, have been defiled by meaningless English impositions. The place name *Kill* for example from the Gaelic *cill* for 'church' and signed in big bold lettering on the Naas triple carriageway in County Kildare, may not only mystify but could even have a disconcerting effect on non-native drivers. The play *Translations* by Brian Friel (1981) exemplifies the absurdity of the practice which started in the late nineteenth century, when Royal engineers arrive in Donegal's *Baile Beag* and, for the purpose of mapping for the Ordnance Survey, attempt to transliterate Gaelic place names and anglicise them.

But there can be a counterpoint to that process too in cities, and there are other place names as in Ciarán Carson's battle-hardened Belfast streets, some of whose names were begot, as David Pierce (2005:250) points out, from imperial ventures in the Crimea and Sevastopol. But in the new Belfast, Carson (2003) tells us in *Exile:* "it is/ as much/ as I can do/ to save/ even one/ from oblivion".

However, there are discernible shifts now in our highly technological age, evident in the poems of Paul Durcan and Paula Meehan who are conscious of the simultaneous presence of alternative modes of perception, like Picasso's figures (q.v.) looking in many directions at once. Picasso proved prophetic for contemporary Western culture with its multitasking, zapping of remote controls to access myriad TV channels and the restlessness of thumbs endlessly text-messaging on mobile phones[2] or Internet cruising, hurling us, as Richard Kearney (Andrews, 1992:48) posits about Kinsella, into the post-modern of experimental 'double coding and collage', and making one wonder if a social single-minded concentration is possible any more (cf. Chap.15.3).

Local place flies away from Durcan (1994) to the global in such poems as *O Westport In The Light of Asia Minor.* And with Meehan (1991) in *The Pattern*

the Liffey for hours pulsing to the sea
and the coming and going of ships,
certain that one day it would carry me
to Zanzibar, Bombay, the land of the Ethiops.

This extension outwards by Irish poets adds yet another dimension through which to see the world: the European tradition from Baudelaire and Lorca, some of whose Gypsy ballads were translated by both Máire Mhac an tSaoi and Michael Hartnett, while Pearse Hutchinson translated from the Catalan; and the American tradition where the patrimony of Whitman can be discerned in the work of many Irish poets[3] with the shades of Lowell on Heaney, and the modernists of Pound, an acknowledged influence on Kinsella. The Beat poets and Magic Realists of South America surely must be deemed as influences in the poetry of Paul Durcan, while the techniques of Hollywood films and Raymond Chandler are evident in the works of Paul Muldoon. Shifting from the initial guidelines of Walter Benjamin, the experimental and post-modern appear playfully at times in the poetry of Ciarán Carson, particularly in *Belfast Confetti* and *Breaking News* and works in between, including *The Irish For No* which, according to Sarah Broom (2006:170), moves Carson further in his exploration of the manner "in which language can effect a radical transformation in the way we see things". Such poetry revels in the freedom of words to let loose and make strange. In his collection *The Twelfth of Never* (a take on the Orange celebration of the twelfth of July) Carson (1999) subverts Yeats' *The Stolen Child*, showing the fairies as unromantic and cruel

When she returned, it seemed she'd little left to lose:
They'd drawn her teeth and danced the toes off her. They'd
docked her ears.

But is it necessary to adopt a backward look or restrict oneself by place? Derry O'Sullivan (1987), whom I discovered through Eiléan Ní Chuilleanáin's illuminating essay, *Borderlands of Irish Poetry* (Andrews, 1992), would seem to think otherwise. He lives in Paris, writes in Gaelic and has translated his own poems into English, making him appear to exist in a dislocated ambiguity. In his poem, *Cá bhFuil do Iúdás* (Where is your Judas?), Judas is a *double entendre* referring not only to the distrust and betrayal of a city but also to a judas window acting as a spying eye

> i gcathair go mbíonn tosaíocht
> ag amhras ar mhuinín
> go minic bíonn an chéad teangmháil
> ar sceabha faoi scrúdú
> leathshúile dofheicthe
>
> In a city where mistrust
> Is a primal reflex
> The first contact often comes down to
> One invisible spying eye.

If translations, as Dennis O'Driscoll (1991:16) suggests, tumble out of the printing presses "like bricks from the Tower of Babel", then all the better, as it brings the universal vision closer – "the vision at last" that Krapp discovered in *Krapp's Last Tape* (Beckett, 1958), drawing us towards a world where there will be no foreigners any more.

This looking out is also reflected in the poetry of Nuala Ní Dhomhnaill who also manages to look backwards and forwards simultaneously, having spent some years in Turkey married to a Turk. She tells us how her learning of Turkish from her father-in-law brought her back to Gaelic

> Living *a la Turca* for five years at an early age made me something akin to an anthropologist (cf. Heaney). It was sharpened by feeling myself at home in a language so entirely different from Irish, and paradoxically, helped me focus more and than ever on Irish. Being outside an English-speaking world for so long also made me aware of my other mother-language. This all came to me from learning Turkish (*The Poet's Chair*, *2008*:99).

The scope of Ní Dhomhnaill is further extended by the transmogrification of her work by Michael Hartnett and the Northern poet Paul Muldoon, among others, into poems in their own right in English. This process brings poetry beyond borders and out of the monoglot, engendering a new dimension not only in its double vision but also in its dual capability as already alluded to in Hartnett's *Necklace of Wrens*. The colloquial raciness of an original Ní Dhomhnaill poem can still be gleaned from a Muldoon version

> *An Crann*
> do tháinig bean an leasa
> le Black & Decker,
> do ghear sí anuas mo chrann.
> D"fhanas im óinseach ag féachaint uirthi
> faid a bhearraigh sí na brainsí
> ceann ar ceann

> *As For the Quince*
> there came this bright young thing
> with a Black & Decker
> and cut down my quince-tree.
> I stood with my mouth hanging open
> while one by one
> she trimmed off the branches.
> (Fallon:405).

16.2 Animus, anima

Perhaps another duality that could be added to Donoghue's list – I won't say of binary opposition, because in this case I don't believe they should be opposed – is that of the male and female way of seeing. Eavan Boland has made a public issue of this, believing female sensibility was ignored by the established canon. While there were obvious injustices in the past as regards female representation, the most orchestrated perhaps being their scant showing in the first Field Day anthology, I believe such injustices in a literary sense have been rectified,[4] and to continue to go down that road is damaging to art by rendering it gender-based and

political.[5] When one considers the large number of scholarly studies that recently
have appeared on the poetry of Eavan Boland, it renders redundant her perception
of herself as marginalised, indeed making it ironic, as she now enjoys high profile
literary respectability together with a chair in the groves of academe.

   Besides, marginality is not exclusively a female preserve. Stephen Dedalus, as
Gerald Dawe points out (1995:170), suffered while watching his father and his
cronies drinking to their past, and feeling sundered from them. Hélène Cixous
(1972:92) describes such a phenomenon

> the other world is there, accessible to the initiated; to reach beyond
> apparent objectivity, one has to decipher the sign, to use one's eyes in
> order to surprise the double face of things and the double meaning of the
> signs. Thus all developments entail equivocation: the innocent exterior is
> the mask of a delicious perversity.

Outsiderhood (q.v.) which Boland, the daughter of a diplomat, appropriates as a
female condition, we have already alluded to in Louis MacNeice and the above
cited Joyce, and indeed one could make a case for it as a requisite for all artists
(cf. Chap 4.1). And the personal is not a total lacuna either, which Boland seems
to claim, in the chronology of Irish poetry, as it appears in *An Duanaire* poems as
pointed out by Seamus Heaney (q.v.). As for a female voice, Eibhlín Ní
Chonaill's lament *Ag Caoineadh Airt Uí Laoghaire* is hailed by Peter Levi (*The
Poet's Chair*:65) as the greatest poem written on these islands in the eighteenth
century, and deemed one of the greatest laments and love poems of all time by
Nuala Ní Dhomhnaill. And potent female protagonists can wittily be heard in
Merriman's *The Midnight Court* and indeed, as Declan Kiberd avers, in many of
Yeats" "strong-willed" women. Also, Seán O'Casey's plays, as Brigitte Bastiat
(2007:54) informs us, give women "a clear and powerful voice" And, nearer the
present, it could be noted that the declared veneration of Edna O'Brien for James
Joyce does not detract in any way from the strong feminine perspective in her
works.

Additionally Boland, by believing that myths are best dismantled from within, thus making her stick to the notion of the nation state, brings her into difficulties with some critics such as Edna Longley and other women writers who have a problem with the term "Mother Ireland", and they accuse Boland of reinstating some of the clichés which she set out to question in the first place (Kiberd, 1996: 607). [6]

Indeed, as Katie Donovan (1988) in her pamphlet, *Irish Women Writers: Marginalised by Whom?* points out, writers such as Joyce Carol Oates find it annoying and restricting to be categorised as a Woman's Writer, fearing that "the only works of mine analysed being those that deal explicitly with women's problems – the rest of my books (in fact the great majority of my books) ignored, as if they had never been written". And Donovan cites Nuala Ní Dhomhnaill who refuses to be declared a feminist, because she feels she could be used in a disputation; and it is Virginia Woolf who reminds us: "The essential difference lies in the fact, not that men describe battles and women the birth of children, but that each sex describes itself."

Eavan Boland (1986) asserts that new language to her is like a "scar", a wound that will heal. The real scar, I believe, that tends to take from her poetry lies in her polemic, which appears to colonise her at times (cf. Marcuse, q.v.), and which seems to imply that Irish society is merely oogamous and must be resisted. Writing in this manner could undermine the artistic value of some of her work for going beyond social concern into the realm of what some could interpret as AGITPROP (cf. Chap 12,). And when carried on this wave, her words sometimes may appear imperious and condescending: "I have the truth" (*Object Lessons*), or "I wrote like that once" (*Is it Still the Same*), referring to the younger poets, could be interpreted as constituting arrogance and self importance on her part, what Wills (2002:12) queries as "overweening pride". And lines such as "we are too late. We are always too late" (*Outside History*) could smack, as Sarah Broom (2006:119) posits, of "almost self-indulgent grief", making Broom feel that "there is a sense, sometimes that the elegiac position has been too complacently and too easily established".

We have seen already throughout this work how sharp a commentator Boland is on the human predicament, and when divested of agenda, she can show herself as truly visionary. Experience, for example, the poignancy of universal loss if one interprets "woman" as a synecdoche for "human being" in the non-patriarchal free verse (q.v.) of Boland's (1994) lines

> An ageing woman
> finds no shelter in language.
> She finds instead
> Single words she once loved
> Such as "summer" and "yellow"
> And "sexual" and "ready"
> Have suddenly become dwellings
> For someone else –
> Rooms and a roof under which someone else
> Is welcome, not her.
> (from *Anna Liffey*)

Apart from being a contradiction in itself, art is too important for our world to attempt to divide it by gender. We need to try to see in our mortal humility with our masculine and feminine eyes, to snatch something of Kavanagh's "passionate transitory" from what Kinsella calls "the streaming away of lifeblood, timeblood" (*Technical Supplement*, poem no. XIX) for the task in hand, which is the venturing into the abyss of ourselves for the making of the poems, those "swaying rope ladders across fuming oblivion" (Montague, 1984, from *Process*). The feminine and masculine, the Jungian animus and anima are ingrained in us all as a duality. And in particular, as regards the poets, let us remind ourselves that it was because of the accusation of their being effeminate that Plato banished them from his ideal republic, and we have already seen how some adolescent boys perceive poets as cissies in *The Bridges of Madison County*. So I contend that this dual make-up in our psyche is another Artesian well (cf. Montague, q.v.), perhaps twig- and leaf-covered as regards some of us, but which needs to be drawn from in our common humanity.

Nuala Ní Dhomhnaill (Donovan, 1988) succinctly sums it up: "... the personal input and the personal talent are ultimately what count." She adds that the future is "ours" and she continues: "By ours I mean the female voice, the feminine voice, whether it is men or women who have it."

16.3 The Vision at last

And so equipped with these dualities of vision, and with the rooting out of censorship from Irish society and the decline in church influence and the contemporary widening of cultures through education and travel, and particularly through the Internet (it does have some merits), one could say perhaps that Irish poetry has achieved at last what Eamon Grennan hails as its possible "comprehensive autonomy" (Dorgan:105). Consider one of the new poets, Sinéad Morrissey, influenced by Lorca (*Poeta en Nueva York*) confronting the post 9/11 dilemma in America, a country she perceives as a wounded giant in her poem, *Wound Man*

> Had you survived, Federico...
> would you know what has happened here...?
> I see the Wound Man walking...
> He's been badly hit...
> And yet he rears. Sturdy and impossible. Strong.
> Loose in the world. And out of proportion.
> (Guinness, 2004:218)

NOTES

[1] It is interesting to note here how in a somewhat similar vein the clergyman Patrick Prunty (father of Emily and Charlotte), on transferring his family from Northern Ireland to England during the Napoleonic era, changed his surname to the more exotic Brontë.

[2] Selina Guinness (2004:29), in her interpretation of Justin Quinn's poem *Fuselage*, suggests that "our sense of individual identity is a necessary illusion as our limbs become adjuncts to the remote control". And Carol Ann Duffy (2005) in her poem *Text*, posits the irony of isolation in the midst of a surfeit of technological communication: 'Nothing my thumbs press/ will ever be heard.'

[3] Eamon Grennan (Dorgan:95-98) points out that even Yeats credits Whitman with turning the Irish poet away from colonial provincialism towards imaginative independence, and that Padraic Fallon acknowledged William Carlos Williams for turning his poetry into a "normal human range", while Patrick Kavanagh humbly expressed gratitude to Gertrude Stein for breaking up "the cliché formation of my thought".

[4] In 2002 Field Day published their fourth and fifth volumes devoted to writing on and by Irish women. It should also be pointed out that there were journals which did welcome women writers in the "maligned" sixties and earlier, such as *The Dublin Magazine* which published, among others, Leland Bardwell, Anne Cluysenaar, Eithne Strong and Mary Lavin. The latter is recognised as one of the foremost practitioners of the short story form and was elected Saoi of Aosdána in 1992. And in her writing against her well documented "absurd authority", she is surely a worthy precursor to Eavan Boland. Lavin published her collection *In The Middle of the Fields* in 1967, and of her earlier collection *Tales from Bective Bridge* (1943) she wrote

> The stories in it were accepted one after the other as they were written, by magazines of repute – *The London Mercury, The Dublin Magazine* and similar publications. They were quickly collected in book form, for which Lord Dunsany wrote a preface. The book was awarded the James Tait Black Memorial Prize, reviewers were unanimously kind to it, and it became a Readers' Union choice which made it a commercial as well as a literary success.

As regards contemporary Ireland, it could be argued that in some cases it is the male writer, particularly the neophyte, who is marginalised in the light of the phenomenon of some exclusively female book clubs and literary competitions and prizes, and the increasing number of publications of women-only poetry and short story anthologies. Attic Press and Arlen House (of which Eavan Boland was a founder and which publishes some men), are openly professed feminist publishers, and Poolbeg, which at one time fostered writers such as John McGahern, now refuses to consider contemporary fiction written by males. And the Irish Lyric FM radio station has broadcast a series for women writers only. And also it may be interesting to note in a more global context that Robert Lowell – a cited influence on Heaney – according to the American critic James Longenbach (*Metre, Thirteen*), now more often "appears as a minor, catalysing figure in critical narratives about (Elizabeth) Bishop's career, much as Bishop once appeared as a footnote to Lowell's formal breakthrough".

[5] Even Virginia Woolf entered in her diary (12/05/1929), when she had finished her essay on *Women* and *Fiction*, that she was "eager to be off – to write without any boundary coming slick in one's eyes". And more modernly, the writer Laura Hird (2003), when interviewed in the *Barcelona Review*, echoes a similar feeling: "I don't really think about gender when I'm writing. It can get in the way sometimes. Both men and women can be strong or vulnerable and weak".

[6] In her poem *Mise Éire*, Eavan Boland (1986) attempts to subvert Pádraig Pearse's poem of the same name where Ireland is portrayed as a mother figure. Boland shifts the matrix to garrison prostitute or emigrant mother. In so doing, Wills (1991:158), Meaney (1993:146) and Longley (1994:178), all women writers, believe she is not engaging critically with the notion of nation but is simply stereotyping and replacing one cliché (Mother Ireland) with that of another (Madonna-whore).

[7] Alan Titley informs us (Dorgan:89) that Nuala Ní Dhomhnaill can write in a masculine persona as she did in *Amhrán an fhir óig* just as she can in a female persona as in *Feis*. He points out: "Most of the time it doesn't matter whether it seems to be a woman or a man speaking (cf. Laura Hird, q.v.), she just gets on with being overwhelmed by feeling and expressing it." The idea of mutual male/female interdependability is captured by the Scottish poet, Ian Crichton Smith, in his poem *For Poets Writing in English over in Ireland* (Pierce, 2000: 902) when he reads an old Gaelic poem translated into English about a poet whose spouse had died: "Half of my eyes you were, half of my hearing/ Half of my walking you were, half of my side."

17 SEEING UNFENCED WORLDS

17.1 Building Bridges

Translation is an imperfect art, yet where would civilisation be without it?
Writers such as Aimé Césaire and Carlos Fuentes have publicly warned, that
without cross-cultural understanding, the world is doomed. "Translation is a
bridge between cultures" (Croghan, 1990:9).

A culture that is only introspective is in danger of expunging from the
imagination that which is not within its experience, as if it were non-existent,
perceiving of itself as unalterable or even hegemonic. It is likely to lack the
longing to reach out for that "otherness", which is necessary for world harmony.

Poetry in translation is like a "global satellite" (Weissbort, 1989:12), bringing
the world closer together (cf. Swir: poets as "antennae," q.v.).

It is with such thoughts in mind – and hopefully, in order to advance a little
further some of the points we have made – that I have chosen three non-Engish
poets (cf. Ch.1). With their eyes we shall attempt to see "otherness" in unfenced
worlds.

17.2 Two Spanish Poets

Before looking briefly at some aspects of the poetry of Salinas and Lorca, it is important at this stage to give credit to language where it is due. In the light of Saussure's double articulation principle, it is worth noting that there are only twenty one distinctive units or phonemes in Spanish, and yet these can produce one hundred thousand significant units or monemes – no small achievement. So when we appear to denigrate literal language, it must be taken in context. However, it has to be reiterated, that what the poet is trying to do, is to extend those significant units even further, to cross conventional boundaries of language to see what lies beyond, and to attempt an articulation of the hidden forces in man – the unexpressed, and in some cases the inexpressible.

17.2.1 Pedro Salinas: Poetry in Motion

Ciudad, ¿te he visto o no?
La noche era una prisa
por salir de la noche.
Tú al paso me ofreciste
gracias vagas, en vano
(*Pasajero apresurado*).

City, have I seen you or not?
the night was in haste
to depart from its darkness.
You in passing offered me
blurred delights, in vain
(*Hurried Passenger*).

Pedro Salinas, unlike many poets, was initially at home with the motor car, and he liked to travel at speed in his fiat 400 through cities, delighting in the fleeting images such activity afforded. He believed that the world and man's mind are in constant motion, and consequently, man's grasp of reality is random and mutable, depending on one's perspective. Thus Bachelard's theory of *Approximates* (q.v.) is not unlike Salinas' relativism, and both men are suspicious of rationality, which they considered rather static.

In *Pasajero apresurado* (Salinas, 1975:111), we witness a fragmented vision from a moving car: a misted cathedral; water illuminated from bridges; a flower guarded by glass, "the heart of shops"; "a shapely calf in a fine stocking" (is fetishisation of body parts prompted by motility?); and "the asphalt offering a dirty mercury to the clouds". Such a kinetic view of reality, to Salinas, is an indication of man's visual limitations.[1]

Perceiving reality in motion, also mobilises the reader to join in the journey with the poet. The city is such a vast reality, we cannot hope to perceive it all, but with Salinas at the wheel, we can glimpse some of it by surrendering ourselves in sympathy to the aspects of itself which it presents to us (cf. Bergson's "sympathetic coincidence"). As Calvino (Tocci, 1994:37) puts it: the city's dialogue changes "from act to act".

We have already indicated that our minds do not travel in a linear fashion, but by using the art that is required to lose oneself in cities, we can subject ourselves to an illumination or an epiphany: "Los mapas falsos,/ trastornando las rumbas" (p.254) ("Maps are false and put us off course"). Walter Benjamin (1992a:298), in *A Berlin Chronicle*, expresses a similar idea

> Not to find one's way about in a city is of little interest... But to lose one's way in a city, as one loses one's way in a forest, requires practice... I learned this art late in life: it fulfilled the dreams whose first traces were the labyrinths on the blotters of my exercise books.

Salinas' poetry is random and spontaneous; it attempts to "extraviadamente... acertar" ("to hit the mark by going astray"). It is reminiscent of Bécquer who described poetry as a "flying arrow shot at random, not knowing where it will come to rest." One must surrender to its flight. As Salinas says in his *Poetica* (Havard, 1988:192): "Hay que dejar que corra la aventura, con toda esa belleza de riesgo, de probabilidad, de jugada" ("One must let the adventure run with all that beauty of risk, of probability and play"). In order to see, we need different perspectives. An orange, as Ortega avers (1963:333), can never be perceived whole, and its juice remains invisible; or as Salinas puts it: "el secreto se defiende dentro" ("its secret is guarded within"). Seeing reality from different perspectives is also interesting from the point of view of painting (at which Salinas was also gifted), for, as Havard points out (p.152), many of Picasso's paintings depict a figure simultaneously in fullface and in profile; in other words they attempt to see the "orange" whole.[2]

Touching is also important for the poet in comprehending reality (cf. Tomlinson, q.v.). In a dark room he touches a lemon, which he cannot see, and he becomes aware of an aspect of its essence: "Te tengo en las manos,/limpio limón escondido,/limpio limón descubierto" (p.80) ("I have you in my hands/clean hidden lemon/clean discovered lemon"). This is not unlike Francisco X. Alarcón's description of poems as "oscuras piedras que al chocar dan luz" ("dark stones that give light when struck") (Rich, 1993:223) — the emphasis being on the striking. Jorge Luis Borges (1964), referring to Berkeley, expresses a not dissimilar idea (cf. intertextuality), suggesting that reality only comes alive by our interconnection with it

> The taste of the apple (states Berkeley) lies in the contact of the fruit with the palate, not in the fruit itself; in a similar way poetry lies in the meeting of poem and reader, not in the lines of symbols printed on pages of a book. What is essential is the thrill, the almost physical emotion that comes with each reading.

Such a thrill, we can sense in the company of Salinas, as he drives us at breakneck speed through city streets, giving us what Havard (p.158) calls "snapshots" of reality.

The cinema also had quite an influence on the poet. Like the rectangle of the window of his house, which divided reality for him into four squares, similarly, the rectangle of the cinema screen is harsh, until moving images are projected onto it; and then it transforms to "dulzura... ondulación" ("sweetness...a wave") (*Cinemátografo*).

However, despite what we said earlier about the marvels of language, for a purist like Salinas, words eventually became inadequate to express his art. Like Paz, or Clare, he wanted to release words from their bondage. Like Joyce, he wanted words that were at the same time "suspiros y risas, colores y notas" (p.253) ("sighs and laughter, colours and notes"). In *La voz a ti debida*, he attacks the restricting effect of naming. If Wednesday had no name, or the seasons, or his beloved, he would have to invent anew and, like Paz, he would attempt to discover everything pristine once more. Or again, like Paz, in *¡Qué gran víspera el mundo!* (*What a great eve is the world!*), he tries to escape history by asking his beloved why the past could not be called a "star" or a "humming bird," in order to "quitarle su veneno" ("extract its poison"). In his constant quest to "hit the mark," he destabilises language, and in one poem tries to resist the connotative function of nouns (cf. Hopi), by writing a love poem in which he extols pronouns: "¡Qué alegría más alta:/vivir en los pronombres!... Te quiero pura, libre,/irreductible: tú!" (p.243) ("What great joy to live in pronouns/I love you pure, free, irreducible: you"). Again like Joyce, perhaps we could say Salinas tested language to its limits, and found it wanting.

However, he need not have felt disillusioned; for, by way of his linguistic experimentation, and his poetically-constructed "deictic shifters," he opened poetry out, and allowed poetry to open us out (as readers), to the grasping of different structures,[2] and thus to the gaining of other perspectives of worlds.

NOTES

[1] Charles P. Steinmetz (1923), in *Four Lectures on Relativity and Space*, showed that when a train moves, the measurement of it by the observer will change, whereas the passenger's measurement will remain consistent with its stationary length (Bradford, p.72).

[2] The artist is always trying to discommode our customary ways of seeing in order to force a new vision. Herman Helmholtz pointed out, as far back as 1894 that

> we tend to favour certain ways of using our sense organs – those ways which provide us with the most reliable and most consistent judgements about the forms, spatial relations, and properties of the objects we observe (Gregory: 309).

However, he goes on to suggest that "unusual perceptions" which occur "with unusual positions and movements of our sense organs, can lead to "incorrect interpretations." I would like to point out that perceptions are not dogmas – Helmholtz himself even refers to them as "inferences" – and to suggest that one way of seeing is "normal" and more correct than another, is of no great help to the artist. Society tends to choose the "normal" vision, not because it is correct, but because it is the most *comfortable* with which to live (cf. Chs.4.1, 15.3 & 17:N[6]).

[3] Bruner (pp.66-7) points out that a child's mastery of "deictic shifters," is indicative, not of egocentrism, but of a failure to grasp the structures of events that leads him to adopt an egocentric framework.

17.2.2 Federico García Lorca: The Hidden Dream

The early, magical ritual of poetry is conjured up by Lorca in his 1932 lecture on *Poeta en Nueva York* when he says, that to understand the metaphors in his poetry, one must invoke the *duende* (*the spirit*), and as for him, he can explain nothing, and I translate, "but stammer with the fire that burns inside me". (Colección Austral, 1990:168)

In the introduction to this work, we mentioned the dual concealment in Lorca's poetry: the hidden grammar of poetry itself, and also the hiding of his own sexual orientation. This latter problem reached a crisis stage for him, when in 1929, he embarked for New York. It was a dark night of the soul for the poet, reminiscent of San Juan de la Cruz without the hope.[1] One device that Lorca exploited – in both his plays and poetry – to hide his own sexuality, was to express his frustrations through the lips of sexually-repressed Andalusian women. In the dream-like *Soledad,* for example, the eponymous woman comes down from the mountain, not wishing her "muslos de amapola" ("poppy thighs") to waste away, and in her quest for sexual fulfilment, suffers the same agonies as Lorca himself. He uses exclamation marks frequently to indicate his unfulfilled desires: *In La Monja Gitana* (*The Gypsy Nun*), a nun will be enclosed in a barren convent for her sexual sins, and the "¡Ay Dios qué grave cosa!" ("O God, what a grave thing!") is repeated a number of times. He was tormented by his inability to express what was a taboo subject in Catholic Spain: "Por qué nací entre espejos?" ("Why was I born between mirrors?") he asks in *Canción del Naranjo Seco* (*Song of the Dry Orange Tree*). The horse is a frequent symbol of male virility in his poetry. *In Romance Sonámbulo* (*Sonambulist Ballad*), we find: "El barco sobre el mar/ el caballo en la montaña" ("The ship on the sea/the horse on the mountain"), the ship, being a symbol for the female sexual organ. In *Intermedio* "los gatos se comían a las ranas" ("cats consumed the frogs") was a euphemism he heard as a child for cats copulating. His longing for the innocence of childhood would remind one of the Gaelic poet, Máirtín Ó Díreáin (q.v.), whose poetry in essence is childhood remembered.

However, the dark hallucinatory poetry of Lorca's American sojourn is terrifying and surreal. For the poet, to transfer from rural Andalusia to the city of New York, was a culture shock. He identified with the downtrodden, especially the Blacks, whom he observed abandoned in alleyways eating their straw hats. As Havard points out (p.221), "comer paja" ("to eat straw") is Granada slang for masturbation. The plight of the poor, Lorca saw as hopeless, in the hungry twenties.

We have already referred to the moon in Lorca's poetry, but in his New York poems, this symbol for poets is not just tainted, but totally defiled. A random sample in translation: "The moon was in a sky so cold/that she had to tear open her mound of Venus," or "the moon was a horse's skull," or "the moon's light escaped from a wound," or "the moon destroyed." In contrast to Salinas, who delighted in the city's motility, Lorca — as he expressed it in his lecture — felt so alienated in an uncaring city that he said: "if you fall into the water they will bury you under their lunch wrappers" (p.174). Ironically, for poetry which is about a city, *Poeta en Nueva York* abounds in references to nature; but it is nature contorted and debased: "Hay nodrizas que dan a los niños/ríos de musgo" (*El Niño Stanton*) ("There are wetnurses who give their children rivers of moss") (*The Child Stanton*). In *Navidad en el Hudson* (*Christmas on the Hudson*): "Cantaba la lombriz el terror de la rueda" ("The earthworm sang its terror of the wheel"). In *Crucifixión*, the moon strikes back in a surreal manner: "Y llegaban largos alaridos por el Sur de la noche seca./Era que la luna quemaba con sus bujías el falo de los caballos?" ("And long screams came from the South in the arid night./It was the moon with its candles burning the phallus of the horses"). But in *Luna y Panorama de los Insectos* (*Moon and Panorama of the Insects*), the moon has been destroyed by the maninsects swarming all over it, suffocating it, blackening the white glow of the Host

Los insectos solos,
crepitantes, mordientes, estremecidos, agrupados, y
la luna
con un guante de humo sentada en la puerts de sus
derribos.

Only the insects
crackling, biting, shaking, thronging,
and the moon
with a glove of smoke seated at the door of its
destruction.

Nature is abused as evidenced by the artificially bloated roses, which he witnessed in New York; and in a scene from his short film script *El Paseo de Buster Keaton* (*Buster Keaton's Ride*), he says: "la maquina Singer puede circular entre las grandes rosas de los invernaderos" ("the Singer sewing-machine can blend with the huge roses of the glasshouses"). The song of the Singer sewing-machine, as Havard points out (p.223), is a crude allusion to female masturbation. In America, in Lorca's eyes, anything goes. Beauty and delicacy are destroyed. In the poem, *Nueva York*, he says: "Y los trenes de rosas maniatadas/por los comerciantes de perfumes" ("And the trains of roses handcuffed by perfume traders"). At the end of that poem he juxtaposes man-made superficialities with the deeply primeval: "esas oficinas... que borran los programas de la selva" ("those offices which wipe out the plans of the forest"), "y el Hudson se emborracha de aceite." ("and the Hudson gets drunk on oil"); and in *Vaca* (*Cow*) "el agua que no desemboca" ("the water that never flows out"): "Agua fija en un punto,/suspirando on todos sus violines sin cuerdas/en la escala de las heridas y los edificios deshabitados" ("water, static in one place, breathing with all its violins, stringless on the scale of wounds and uninhabited buildings").

America offers no hope for Lorca, even the "marvellous light" which the school teachers show the children in *Grito hacia Roma* (*Cry towards Rome*), is "una reunión de cloacas" ("a joining of sewers"). This dark night of screaming "con la cabeza llena de excremento" ("with heads full of excrement") only heightened the already crippling, sexual crisis in the poet. He identified closely with Walt Whitman, not only sexually, but also in his love of nature: the wide open plains of America, in contrast with "Nueva York de cieno/ Nueva York de alambre y de muerte" ("New York of mire/New York of wire and death"). In his *Oda a Walt Whitman* (*Ode to Walt Whitman*), Lorca is at his most explicit sexually. He sees in Whitman someone to emulate, one whose homosexuality was manly, noble, and overt, unlike the furtive, effeminate homosexuals whom he invokes by the pejorative names, which society has assigned them: "Fairies de Norteamerica,/ Pájaros de La Habana,/Jotos de Méjico" etc. Whitman's confidence inspires Lorca to step tentatively out of the closet, to state openly that: "Puede el hombre, si quiere, conducir su deseo/ por vena de coral o celeste desnudo" ("Man is capable if wants, to drive his desire through a vein of coral or blissful nakedness").

Even our brief look at Lorca's poetry helps us to appreciate how he conjured up, magically as it were, from the deep recesses of dreams or nightmare, a new way of seeing. He showed us an aspect of the orange from a different side, digging deeply to find fresh symbols to express in poetry what he could not express openly.

Lorca's poetry, apart from its intrinsic beauty, helps us to see what we, as human beings, are doing to the world, and to each other, and in particular, what we are doing, to what Frank O'Connor called "submerged population groups": the Blacks, with whom Lorca identified, not only because they were downtrodden, but also because they shared natural musical rhythms with his fellow Andalusians; the gypsies, with whom the poet felt a deep kinship; and, of course, he also identified with those, who like himself, were trapped "between two mirrors".

His murder, it could be argued, was motivated as much by homophobia, as it was by any anti-Franco sentiments. Being a true artist, he was essentially apolitical. By studying his poetry, perhaps the human race could be a little more tolerant of each other.

NOTES

[1] It is interesting to record that San Juan de la Cruz, like Lorca, also had to write in coded language because, similar to Santa Teresa de Ávila, it was claimed that he had some Jewish blood, and thus he feared the Inquisition. The parallel could be continued if one looked upon Franco's *Guardia Civil* as Lorca's inquisitors. Ironically, it was a code, used by the latter, that ordered the shooting of Lorca. "Give him coffee," was General Queipo de Llano's coded command for the execution of the poet (cf. Matthew Sweeney's poem on Lorca in his collection, *Cacti* {1992}).

17.3 Boris Pasternak: Pristine Vision

(Translations from Pasternak are by J. Stallworthy and P. France — 1984).

"A branch splashes white lace on the window. Is there a witness?" Pasternak was the witness, a poet of intense sensitivity who blended his thoughts with birdsong, and painted word-pictures of snowy Russian landscapes so lyrically moving that he brought a simplicity back to poetry at a time when others were trying to complicate it. The crystal precision of Pasternak's writing, as Levi (1991:195) points out, is based on synaesthesia: intense perceptions based on an intermingling with childhood memories and observations. Having been brought up with ears and eyes open to the music and painting of his mother and father respectively (she was a famous pianist, and he, among other works, illustrated Tolstoy's *Resurrection*), Pasternak applied these senses in a heightened fashion to his perceptions of the world. For those of us who do not know Russian, we lose a string in the violin. Take for example, *In Hospital*, where a dying man sees from an ambulance "militsia, ulitsa, litsa" ("police, streets, faces"), one doesn't need Russian to realise that the thickly-woven sound pattern is lost in translation. Pasternak himself was renowned as a translator, particularly of Shakespeare, and he stated (1984:12) that "the principal charm of a work of art lies in its unrepeatability" (cf. Benjamin's *aura*, q.v.). However, he appreciated the utility of translation "not as a method of getting to know isolated works... but as a channel whereby cultures and peoples communicate down the centuries" (cf. Croghan, q.v.).

Thus we proceed with one string missing; nevertheless, what a feast lies in store. Witness his description of unnamed lightning in one of his many portraits of a storm: "The storm at night for souvenir/Took snap after dazzling snap;" or after rain: "the slugs in the garden will plug the eyes of statues;" or the stars growing so low, and midnight falling "to the feather-grassed ground," and "muslin-mist" thirsting "for the grand finale to sound;" or the Steppe steeped in snow "is tonight as before the Fall:/All lapped in peace, all like a parachute./A rearing vision all."

Pasternak, like Ortega and Salinas, realised that all of reality could not be described. He looked upon his role as similar to that of an impressionist painter. His "brush" was metaphor, which he described as the "shorthand of the soul"

> And suddenly here it is written
> Again, in the first snow — the spidery
> Cursive italic of sleigh runners —
> A page like a piece of embroidery.
> (*Winter Approaches*)

His poetry is so much in harmony with nature, that it actually becomes nature

> I should plant out my stanzas.
> And flowering limes,
> Their veins astir with sap,
> Would bloom in lines.
> (*When the Weather Clears*)

Such intensity of delight (the triumph of blooming in lines) "tightens the bowstring,/bending the bow" (cf. Yeats' description of the intense beauty of Maud Gonne "like a tightened bow"). We, like the trees observed, are filled with sap, with life, as if his poetry combined with a lightning flash to energise us, and enable us to observe the world anew with heightened consciousness.

The vision in Pasternak's poetry is so pure, so pristine that we feel we are witnessing — what Paz and Salinas and Clare sought but never found — the world as it was at the Creation. We see a mountain, as if for the first time, when we look with Pasternak's eyes, or hear a storm raging, or smell the scent, as raindrops fill the cups of flowers.

It is commonly known that snow falls frequently in Russia, yet each snowfall, described by Pasternak, is the original, as if the universe were unfolding itself to us for the first time. Even domesticated plants reach out for a wider, freer world

Snow is falling, snow is falling.
Reaching for the storm's white stars,
Petals of geraniums stretch
Beyond the window bars.
(*Snow Is Falling*)

Like the lightning which illuminates distant corners ("when the light is now intense"), Pasternak's poetry lights up our minds, enabling us to see what otherwise would frequently pass unnoticed (cf. Ch.14). Rain can never be the same again after reading Pasternak: "Rain streams down so quietly as though it were light/As though it were the secret of its freedom." In April the "adolescent park simmers". With him, we hear "the murmur of wet roofs,/Faint eclogues of pavement and kerb;" and the soul falls "like a ripe pear into the storm," integrating man, as perhaps no other poet has done, totally and unequivocally with nature, or perhaps more accurately, proclaiming man as nature. In a letter to his father in 1917, he explained that he wished to write about

> ...living feelings, the kind that tangibly pervade the world of human beings, as airy vapours penetrate overgrown gardens and meadows in summer, at midday, after a thunderstorm... such feelings, which everyone carries within himself and embodies in his own life... entrusted to the care of all mankind.
> (from Introduction to *Selected Poems* by Stallworthy & France,1984:23).

He was well aware of the sacrificial nature of the artist's calling, and considered those who observed and wrote about war from the rear or the sidelines as immoral (cf. Heaney's *The Government of the Tongue* q.v. in both meanings of the phrase, or the War Poets, and their idea of having to earn or suffer the right to speak). Pasternak retained his integrity to the end, never once distorting his true voice, something which he could easily have done in Soviet Russia. With the Italian publication of *Doctor Zhivago* (1957) in particular (a work which could be described as an epic poem),[1] he refused to compromise about his critical depiction of the Russian Revolution, and he paid the price for Art. He prophesied his own

martyrdom: "I know I shall be tied/onto a wooden post." In *Nobel Prize* (a prize
he was forced to decline in 1958) he exclaims

> Like a beast in a pen, I'm cut off
> From my friends, freedom, the sun,
> But the hunters are gaining ground.
> I've nowhere else to run.

He wished to live hidden from his persecutors, his life "not a poet's but a poem",
condemned for making "the whole world weep at the beauty of my land". He
cried for help, just "for one second", but there was no hand long enough to reach
out to him at the end. Pasternak renewed our sense of wonder of the world. His
apparently lyrical simplicity belied the agonising efforts of a true artist who
enabled us to see the world as a place of great beauty. Perhaps if we were to take
down his life from the shelf and blow the dust from his name, we might pause,
before engaging in activities, which could corrupt the purity of his vision.

NOTES

[1] It was thought by some critics that Pasternak made Yuri Zhivago a doctor in homage to Chekhov, whom he admired. However, it is also interesting to note the interconnectedness of science/poetry in Yuri as doctor/poet (cf. Bachelard). Pasternak tells us that he spent twenty years preparing *Doctor Zhivago*, and that it was his most important work. The whole book is, in essence, a reflection on the role of the poet and of poetry in the world, as well as being, in the eyes of some, a poem in itself. Some critics maintain that the poems to Lara at the end of the novel are superior to the novel in its own right. I believe, however, that Pasternak wanted it all to blend – prose, poetry, science – into a great symphony of the world. For him, *Doctor Zhivago* was the summation of all his art, and it is on that broad basis the work should be judged.

18 CONCLUSIONS AND DISCUSSION

18.1 A Look to the Future

We have already outlined some causes of future concern for society, and for poetry in particular, in relation to education, literary magazines etc., and with the use of the CD-ROM now, some critics even prophesy the death of the book itself.

Worrying also is Jean-Michel Guy's (1994:9) prognostication of an Americanised Europe, in which the "average" Dane or Portuguese have nothing more to share than the American programmes they watch on television.

Bearing in mind the global, cultural influence of America, this concern becomes particularly disquieting, when one considers, that in the U.S. the study of criticism, *sui generis*, has now usurped that of poetry, with the result that verse is read much less now than prose narrative (Princeton:ix) (cf. Ch. 12.2).[1] Thus it may said that poetry, in some cases, has been reduced to what Crozier (Sinfield, 1983:229) calls "a daring little frill round the hem of normal discourse" (cf. Rich's "garnish").

Another area of concern has to do with publishers themselves. As we have already seen in the case of John Clare, there is nothing new in publishers seeking profitability. However, it would appear, that when 100,000 pounds could be advanced for a Naomi Campbell "novel" (when most artists are impoverished {cf.

Ch.15:N[3]}), the gap is closing between what is perceived as meritorious and meretricious.[2]

Nevertheless, all is not gloomy. The CD-ROM, for example, affords local access to the world's libraries.[3] And Peter Sirr (1994:7) informs us that the Internet has prepared audio clips of poets reading from their work, accompanied by photographs and critical biographies of the poets. This is very useful, particularly for schools and colleges, and for distance-learning.

Also, poetry CDs are proving increasingly popular, and could have a therapeutic effect, for example, when played in traffic jams (one technology, attempting, as it were, to make amends for the damage done by another {cf. Ch.13}). And the Japanese have even found an answer for the writer who prefers the pen to the word processor: a colour computer-screen that can be rolled up into a pen (*Irish Times*, 22/2/95).

So it appears, that just as we have seen with the evolution of visual and concrete poems, poets themselves have to adapt to the new technology (it will not go away[4]), and create new forms,[5] because poetry, as Louis MacNeice has said, "*has* to matter" (my italics). In the words of Holub (p.132), a poem, "in its desperate commitment to the word, in its primal order of birth and re-birth, remains the most general guarantee that... we can still *do* something against emptiness".

David Constantine (1989), elaborating on such a view, sums up the contemporary situation

> Contemporary verse, whether it will last or not, has peculiar importance in that it shows what we face today, it shows what *might* be done, it discovers our truth: the harsh facts we *might* be capable of. In nihilistic, mercenary and cynical times poetry is a ground and means of opposition. It can persuade you of two things simultaneously: that there is something worth fighting for, and that the fight has not yet been lost.

18.2 Conclusions

In this work I tried to show poetry as an alternative and enriching way of looking at the world. We examined some of its grammar, and saw, hopefully, how it helps us to gain some understanding of our non-rational selves – parts of ourselves which we ignore at our peril. In this context it is interesting to note how we sometimes label the poet as an "oddity", to avoid feeling threatened by the disturbing power of his poems.[6]

Again hopefully, we caught a glimpse of how the freshness of poetry can liberate language, can renew our metaphors, which we have seen are an important mechanism in the human communication system.

In poetry, the word can be made to "sparkle", as Barthes (1967:37) says, "with infinite meaning, and is ready to radiate towards a thousand uncertain and possible relations".

By widening our insight into reality, poetry can lead us to deeper dialogues about the world and man's place in it.

Poetry strips away heavily encrusted layers of time, and helps us to see the world fresh and pristine, restoring our faith in life.

Poetry, like all art, is anarchic, and yet can be deeply spiritual, and in some cases, can usurp the role of religion or oppressive ideologies. Whether it will go as far as Matthew Arnold prophesied, however, is questionable i.e., that it would actually "replace" philosophy and religion. Nevertheless, there is no doubt that an agnostic age can endow poetry with an urgent impetus, as it attempts to find meaning, spiritual and otherwise, in the chaos surrounding us.

One of poetry's attractions is that it is free. It cannot be restrained. Witness, for example, the multiplicity of attempted definitions of poetry, none of which is comprehensive. It defies definition. It is airy and flies away, which is another reason why, despite the value of much of their work, I disagree with the Structuralists. Poetry cannot be contained within logical confines.

Poetry helps us to fill gaps in our lives. As readers, we enter a poem's world with our own experiences and expectations, and seek fulfilment by attempting to fill in the gaps left by the poet in the poem; and the poet, for his part, seeks plenitude by creating art.

Literal language, for the most part, like so much in our consumer society, is disposed of as soon as it is used. Poetic language, however, lives on, retaining its vigour for a long time.

As well as liberating language, poetry also enables us to question presumptions which have built up over time in our tongues. We have already contrasted some of these presumptions in English *vis-à-vis* Hopi, but one need not even travel as far. Contrast the use of possessive adjectives in English and Spanish: In English the possessive is used at every opportunity, e.g. "my coat", "my face". In Spanish (despite its own colonial past, and unless for purposes of emphasis or differentiation) such examples are rendered: "the coat", "the face", as if accepting a commonality. Such rampant usage of possessives in English would seem to suggest an acquisitiveness, as if we want to possess the world. If this is so, then it is in total conflict with the poetic way of seeing our place in the world, which is, as Pasternak says, "as guests of existence" (cf. Clare's commonage).[7]

In his biography of Pasternak, Levi quotes from *Soul*

> It is not earthquake, it is not upheaval
> that leads us to the life of our desire,
> but generosity and open truth,
> and visions in the soul, visions of fire.

Let us go then with "the flock of keys", which are the poems to open cage doors, and remove the bars that obstruct our vision, so that we can see anew.

NOTES

[1] Randall Jarrell compared the intervention of a poet into criticism to the arrival of a pig at a bacon-judging competition. "Go away," the pig was told, "what could you possibly know about bacon?" (O'Brien, 1994b:6) (cf. Ch.1:N[1]).

[2] In Britain, there was an ongoing, legal wrangle involving Reed Publishers, who sacked their poets, because, they claimed, poetry did not make enough money (*Sunday Times*, 11/6/95).

[3] Such ease of access, however, could breed new problems in relation to intellectual property rights.

[4] In his review of R. Hewison's *Culture and Consensus* (1995, Methuen) (*Sunday Times*, 4/6/95), Simon Jenkins cites Konrad Lorenz: "Historians will have to face the fact that natural selection determines the evolution of cultures in the same manner as it did that of species."

[5] Peter Sirr (p.7) admits to stumbling upon *Electric Verse* on the Internet, while in Helsinki. This constitutes new poems by three contemporary Finnish poets, available in Finnish, Swedish and English.

[6] "Art can unnerve when it pushes the boundaries delimited by the public sphere" (Becker: xii) (cf. Helmholtz, q.v.).

[7] Eagleton's summary (p.62) of Heidegger is apt here: "Human existence is in dialogue with the world, and the more reverent activity is to listen rather than to speak."

BIBLIOGRAPHY

ALVAREZ, A. (ed.) (1992) *The Faber Book of Modern European Poetry*.

ANDREWS, E. (ed.) (1992) "Myth and Modernity in Irish Poetry," by Richard Kearney; "Borderlands of Irish Poetry," by Eiléan Ní Chuilleanáin, *Contemporary Irish Poetry: A Collection of Critical Essays*. London: Macmillan.

AN DUANAIRE 1600-1900: *Poems of the Dispossessed*. Dánta Gaeilge curtha i láthair ag Seán Ó Tuama, with verse translation by Thomas Kinsella, Dolmen Press, 1981

ARNOLD, M. (1969) "The Study of Poetry," *Essays in Criticism*. MacMillan.

AUERBACH, E. (1959) *Scenes from the Drama of European Literature*. Manchester UP.

AUSTIN. J. (1962) *How to Do Things with Words*. Oxford: OUP.

BACHELARD, G. (1964) *The Psychoanalysis of Fire*. Trans. A. Ross.Quartet.

---, (1971) *On Poetic Imagination and Reverie*. Indianapolis.

BARTHES, R. (1967) *Writing Degree Zero and Elements of Semiology*. Jonathan Cape.

---, (1984) *Image, Music, Text*. London: Flamingo.

---, (1987) *Criticism and Truth*. London: Athlone Press.

BECKER, C. (ed.) (1994) *The Subversive Imagination: Artists, Society and SocialResponsibility*. Routledge.

BECKETT, S. (1958) "Krapp's Last Tape," *The Complete Plays*. London: Faber, 1990.

BENJAMIN, W. (1973) "The Work of Art in the Age of Mechanical Reproduction," *Illuminations*. Trans. H. Zohn. Fontana.

---, (1992a) *One Way Street And Other Writings*. Trans. E. Jephcott & K. Shorter. London: Verso.

---, (1992b) *Charles Baudelaire: A Lyric Poet in the Era of High Capitalism*. London: Verso.

BERGIN, T.G. & FISH, M.H. (1984) *The New Science of Giambattista Vico*. Ithaca: Cornell UP.

BERGSON, H. (1910) *Time and Free Will*. Trans. F.L. Pogson. London.

BERTHOFF, A. (ed.) (1991) *Richards on Rhetoric: Selected Essays, 1929-74*. Oxford UP.

BLOOM, H. (1976) *Poetry and Repression: Revisionism from Blake to Stevens*. New Haven & London: Yale UP.

BOLAND, E. (1986) "Mise Éire," *The Journey*. Dublin: Arlen House.

---, (1990) "Object Lessons," *Outside History*. Manchester: Carcanet

---, (1994) "A Woman Painted on a Leaf," "The Art of Grief," "Moths," "Love," "Lava Cameo," *In a Time of Violence*. Carcanet.

---, (2001) "Irish Poetry," *Code*. Carcanet.

---, (2003) (ed.) *Three Irish Poets: An Anthology*. Carcanet.

BORGES, J. L. (1964) Quoted from his preface to *Obra poetica 1923 -1964*. Buenos Aires: Emece.

BRADFORD, R. (1993) *The Look of It: A Theory of Visual Form in English Poetry*. Cork Univ. Press.

BRECHT, B. (1987) *Poems 1913-1956*. London: Methuen.

BREWER'S DICTIONARY OF PHRASE & FABLE (1994) 14th ed., revised by I.H. Evans. London: Cassell.

BRINES, F. (1977) *Insistencias en Luzbel*. Madrid: Visor

BRITANNICA, ENCYCLOPAEDIA, 1977 edition. Benton Publishers.

BROOM. S. (2006) *Contemporary British and Irish Poetry*. Palgrave Macmillan.

BRUNER, J. (1986) *Actual Minds, Possible Worlds*. Harvard UP.

BULLOCK, A. & WOODINGS, B. (1983) *The Fontana Dictionary of Modern Thinkers*. London.

BURGER. P. (1992) *The Decline of Modernism*. Cambridge: Polity Press.

CANETTI, E. (1978) *Auto Da Fe*. London: Picador.

CARSON C. (1999) *The Twelfth of Never: Seventy Seven Sonnets*. Picador.

---, (2003) "Exile". *Breaking News*. The Gallery Press. Oldcastle, Co. Meath.

CHESELKA, P. (1987) *The Poetry and Poetics of Jorge Luis Borges*. Peter Lang.

CIXOUS, H. (1972) *The Exile of James Joyce*. New York: David Lewis.

COHEN, J.M. (ed.) (1960) *The Penguin Book of Spanish Verse*.

COLLINS, J. (1989) *Uncommon Cultures*. Routledge.

CONSTANTINE, D. (1989) *The Poetry Book Society Anthology 1988-1989*. London: Hutchinson.

CORMAN, C. (1977) *Word for Word: Essays on the Arts of Language*. Santa Barbara.

CORNWELL, J. (1994) "Hard Raine," *Sunday Times* (magazine), 28/5/94.

CRANE, H. (1930) *The Bridge*. New York: Liveright Publishing.

CROGHAN, M. (1988) "The Language of O'Casey: A Text Analysis of *The Shadow of a Gunman*," *Studies on Sean O'Casey*, ed. J. Genet & W. Hellegouarc'h, Caen: Travaux du Centre de Recherche, 7-22.

---, (1990) "Terms of Address: The Missed Opportunity for Semantics." Ms. from. Dublin City University.

CRONIN, M. (1996) *Translating Ireland: Translation, Languages, Cultures*. Cork University Press.

CULLER, J. (1975) *Structuralist Poetics*. Routledge.

---, (1981) *The Pursuit of Signs*. Routledge.

cummings, e e (1954) *Poems 1923-1954*. NY.

DANESI, M. (1985) "The role of metaphor in cognition," *Semiotica* 77-4 521-531.

DAWE, G. (1995) *Against Piety: Essays in Irish Poetry*. Belfast: Lagan Press.

DAWSON, P.M.S. (1980) *The Unacknowledged Legislator: Shelley and Politics*.

Oxford: Clarendon Press.

DELILLO, D. (1989) *Libra*. Penguin.

---, (1992) *Mao II*. London: Vintage.

DONOGHUE, D. (1987) *We Irish: The Selected Essays of Denis Donoghue*. Brighton: Harvester Press.

DONOVAN, K. (1988) *Irish Women Writers: Marginalised by Whom?* Raven Arts.

---, (1993) "Pattern," *Watermelon Man*. Tarset: Bloodaxe.

DORGAN, T. (ed.) (1996) *Irish Poetry Since Kavanagh*. Four Courts Press.

DUFFY, C.A. (2005) 'Text,' *Rapture*. Picador.

DURCAN, P. (1980) *Jesus, Break His Fall*. Raven Arts.

---, (1994) *Give Me Your Hand*. London: MacMillan.

EAGLETON, T. (1983) *Literary Theory: An Introduction*. Oxford: Basil Blackwell.

ECO, U. (1989) *The Open Work*. Trans. A. Cancogni. London: Hutchinson

ELIOT, T.S. (1953) *Selected Prose* (ed. J. Hayward). Penguin.

---, (1922) *The Waste Land*. New York: Boni and Liveright.

EMANUEL, L. (1992) "The Planet Krypton," *The Dig*. Univ.of Illinois Press.

EMPSON, W. (1961) *Seven Types of Ambiguity*. Penguin.

ESNAULT, G. (1964) *Language & Style*. Trans. S. Ullman. Oxford.

FALLON, P. & MAHON, D. (eds.) (1990) *The Penguin Book of Contemporary Irish Poetry*.

FENOLLOSA, E. (1919) "The Chinese Written Character as a Medium for Poetry," trans. E. Pound. *Prose Keys to Modern Poetry* (ed. K. Shapiro). NY.1962.

FORREST-THOMPSON, V. (1978) *Poetic Artifice: A Theory of Twentieth Centruy Poetry*. Manchester.

FRENCH, M. (1985) *Beyond Power: On Women, Men and Morals*. NY: Ballantine Books.

FREUD. S. (1908) "Creative Writers and Day-Dreaming," *Creativity: Selected Readings* (ed. P.E. Vernon). Penguin, 1980.

FRIEL, B. (1981) *Translations*. Faber.

FRYE, N. (1990) *Selected Essays* (ed. R. Denham). Virginia UP.

GINSBERG, A. (1956) *Howl*. London: Viking.

GREGORY, R.L. (ed.) (1991) *The Oxford Companion to the Mind*. OUP.

---, (1994) *Even Odder Perceptions*. Routledge.

GUINNESS, S. (ed.) (2004) *The New Irish Poets*. Bloodaxe.

GUNN, G. (1987) *The Culture of Criticism and the Criticism of Culture*. OUP.

GUY, J-M. (1994) "The Cultural Practices of Europeans," *The European Journal of Cultural Policy*, vol 1, no 1, pp.3-9.

HAINES, J. (1990) *In the Forest without Leaves, New Poems: 1980-88*. Story Line Press.

HARMON, M. (ed.) (1981) *Irish Poetry After Yeats: Seven Poets*.

Dublin: Wolfhound Press.

HARTNETT, M. (1975) *A Farewell to English*. Dublin. Enlarged edition
The Gallery Press, 1978.

---, (1987) *A Necklace of Wrens: selected poems in Irish with English translations by the author*. The Gallery Press.

---, (2001) "Sibelius in Silence," *Collected Poems*. The Gallery Press.

HAVARD, R. G. (1988) *From Romanticism to Surrealism: Seven Spanish Poets*. Cardiff: Univ. of Wales Press.

HAWKES, T. (1977) *Structuralism and Semiotics*. London: Methuen

HAYWARD, J. (ed.) (1956) *The Penguin Book of English Verse*.

HEANEY, S. (1966) *Death of a Naturalist*. Faber.

---, (1975) "Viking Dublin: Trial Pieces," *North*. Faber.

---, (1988) *The Government of the Tongue*. Faber.

---, (1990) *The Redress of Poetry*. Oxford: Clarendon Press.

HEWISON, R. (1995) *Culture and Consensus*. Methuen.

HIRD, L. (2003) Interview in the *Barcelona Review*, Issue 35: March-April.

HOLUB, M. (1990) *Poems Before & After*. Trans. I.& J. Milner, E. Oners & G. Theiver. Newcastle upon Tyne: Bloodaxe.

HUGHES, T. (1957) *The Hawk in the Rain*. Faber.

HUGHES, T. & Muldoon, P. (1983) *A Faber Poetry Cassette*.

BASTIAT, B. (2007) "Representing Irish Women's Identities in Translation: Women's Movements and Theatre," *International Review of Irish Culture: Ireland in Translation* (Spring). Yorick Libri.

JAKOBSON, R. (1960) "Linguistics and Poetics," *Style in Language* (ed. T. Sebeok). Cambridge: MIT Press.

JONES, M.M. (1990) "On Science, Poetry, and the 'honey of being': Bachelard's Shelley," *Philosophers' Poets* (ed. D. Wood). Routledge.

JOYCE, J. (1927) *Pomes Penyeach*. Faber, 1966.

KAFKA, F. (1954) *Hochzeitsvorbereitungen auf dem Lande*. Trans. Idris Parry. Frankfurt.

KAVANAGH, P. (1984) *The Complete Poems*. Goldsmith Press.

KENNELLY, B. (1991) *The Book of Judas*. Newcastle upon Tyne: Bloodaxe.

KIBERD, D. (ed.) (1991) *The Field Day Anthology*. Derry: Field Day Publications.

---, (1996) *Inventing Ireland: The Literature of the Modern Nation*. Vintage.

KINSELLA, T. (1996) "Baggot Street Deserta," *Collected Poems of Thomas Kinsella*. Oxford Poets.

KOLERS, P.A. (1991) "Imaging," *The Oxford Companion to the Mind* (pp.353-4) (ed. R.L. Gregory). OUP.

KRINO (1990) No. 8/9. (Dublin).

---, (1996) (Dawe, G. & Williams, J. eds.) "Translating Ireland," *Krino 1986-1996: An Anthology of Modern Irish Writing*. (Dublin).

KRISTEVA, J. (1980) *Desire in Language: A Semiotic Approach to Literature &*

Art. Oxford: Basil Blackwell.

---, (1986) "Word, dialogue and novel," *The Kristeva Reader* (ed. Toril Moi). Oxford.

LARKIN, P. (1988) *Collected Poems*. Faber.

LAVIN, M. (1943) *Tales from Bective Bridge*. London: Michael Joseph. Republished, 1978, Dublin: Poolbeg.

LEECH, G.N. (1969) *A Linguistic Guide to English Poetry*. Longman.

LEHMANN, W.P. (1991) "A semiotic approach to oral-formulaic poetry," a review article of Alain Renoir's (1988) *A Key to Old Poems*: *The Oral-formulaic Apprach to the Interpretation of West-Germanic Verse*. Pennsylvania State UP. *Semiotica* 85- 1/2 163-171

LEVI, P. (1991) *The Art of Poetry*. Yale Univ. Press.

---, (1990) *Boris Pasternak*. Hutchinson.

LEVIN, S.R. (1962) *Linguistic Structures in Poetry*. Mouton.

LONGLEY. E. (1994) "From Kathleen to Anorexia: The Breakdown of Irelands," *A Dozen Lips*, 177,180.

LORCA, F. GARCÍA (1929) *Poeta en Nueva York* (ed. Piero Menarini). Colección Austral, 1990.

LOWELL, R. (1961) *For the Union Dead*. Faber.

LYOTARD, J-F. (1984) *The Postmodern Condition: A Report on Knowledge*. Minneapolis: Univ. of Minnesota Press.

MACLEISH, A. (1960) *Poetry and Experience*. Penguin.

MCCRACKEN, K. (1994) Review of Paul Durcan's *Give Me Your Hand* (1994), *Linen Hall Review*, Vol 11, No 3, Winter.

MCDONAGH, J. & NEWMAN, S. (eds.) (2006) "'[B]oth more than a language and no more of *a* language': Michael Hartnett and the politics of translatlion," by Eugene O'Brien. *Remembering Michael Hartnett*. Dublin: Four Courts Press.

MACNEICE, L. (1937) "*Carrigfergus,*" *Collected Poems*. Faber, 2007.

---, (1949) "The Sunlight on the Garden," ibid.

MAHON, D. (ed.) (1972) *The Sphere Book of Modern Irish Poetry*. London: Sphere Books Ltd.

MAJAKOVSKIJ, V. (1925) "Brooklyn Bridge," *The Bedbug and Selected Poetry*. Midland, 1975.

MÁRQUEZ, G. GARCÍA, (1967) *Cien Años de Soledad*. Buenos Aires: Editorial Sudamericana, SA.

MEANEY, G. (1993) "Myth, history and the politics of subjectivity: Eavan Boland and Irish women's writing," *Women: A Cultural Review*, vol. 4, no.2.

MEEHAN, P. (1991) "The Pattern," *The Man Who Was Marked By Winter*. The Gallery Press.

METRE, Thirteen. Winter 2002/2003. University of Hull.

MILLAR, P. (1994) "I am become Death, the destroyer of worlds," *Sunday Times Magazine*, 16/7/95.

MILLER, R. (1994) "Why America killed the Rosenbergs," *Sunday Times Magazine*, 16/7/95.

MILOSZ, C. (1983) *The Witness of Poetry*, Harv. Univ. Press.
---, (1988) *Collected Poems*. Trans. J. Darowski. Penguin.
MININNI, G. (1989) "Metaphor as polilogic semiosis," *Semiotica* 73-3/4, 233-247.
MITCHELL, A. (1985) *On the Beach at Cambridge*. London: Allison & Busby.
MOLE. J. (1989) *Passing Judgements: Poetry in the Eighties*. Bristol.
MONTAGUE, J. (1961) "Poisoned Land," *The Collected Poems*. Wake University Press. Winston, Salem, 1995.
---, (1984) "Process," *The Dead Kingdom*. Dolmen Press.
MONTEFIORE, J. (1983) "Feminist Identity and the Poetic Tradition," *Feminist Review*, no 13.
MOODY, H.L.B. (1968) *Literary Appreciation*. Longman.
MUKAROVSKY, J. (1977) *The Word and Verbal Art: Selected Essays by Jan Mukarovsky* (ed. & trans. by J. Burbank, & P. Steiner). Yale.
NÍ DHOMHNAILL, N. (1988) "Amhrán An Fhir Óig," *Selected Poems: Rogha Dánta* (trans. by Michael Hartnett). Raven Arts.
---, (1991) *Feis*, Má Nuad: An Sagart.
NUESSEL, F. (1992) "Philosophical and metaphorical aspects of language," *Semiotica* 89-1/3 117-128.
O'BRIEN, S. (1994a) "Poetry in Promotion," (Review of the *20 New Generation Poets*), *Sunday Times*, 1/5/94.
---, (1994b) "Reading Between the Lines," (Review of *The Poet's Voice and Craft* {ed. C.B. MCcrully}, Carcanet) *Sunday Times*, 13/2/94.
Ó CADHAIN, M. (1949) *Cré na Cille*. Sáirseal & Dill.
O'DRISCOLL, D. (1991) "In Other Words: A Consideration of Poetry in Translation," *Poetry Ireland Review 31*.
O'MALLEY, M. (1993) "The Shape of Saying," *Where the Rocks Float*. Galway: Salmon Publishers.
ORTEGA Y GASSET, J. (1963) "Meditaciones del 'Quijote,'" *Obras completas* I. Madrid: Espasa Calpe.
Ó SIADHAIL, M. (1994) "Covenants of Trust: The Citizen Poet," *Éire – Ireland*, Fomhar – Fall.
O'SULLIVAN, D. (1987) *Cá bhFuil do Iúdás*. Dublin: Coiscéim. English translation in Derry O'Sullivan, *The King's English*, Paris, 1988.
PASTERNAK, B. (1958) (Eng. ed.) *Doctor Zhivago*. Collins.
---, *Selected Poems*. Trans. J. Stallworthy, & P. France. Penguin. 1984. Pasternak's statements on translation (1944), quoted by his son Yevgeny, from "Notes of a Translator," in the Introduction to *Selected Poems*.
PAULIN, T. (ed.) (1990) *The Faber Book of Vernacular Verse*.
---, (1992) *Minotaur: Poetry and the Nation State*. Faber.
PAZ, O. (1962) *Salamandra*. Mexico City: Joaquín Mortiz.
---, (1970) *Claude Levi-Strauss: An Introduction*. Cornell UP.

PEIG: *Tuairisc a thug Peig Sayers ar imeachtaí a beatha féin* (eagrán scoile de *Machnamh Seanmhná*, 1939) (eag. M. Ní Chinnéide). Comhlacht Oideachais na hÉireann (n.d.).
PERKINS, D. (1987) *A History of Modern Poetry*. Harvard U.P.
PIERCE, D. (ed.) (2000) *Irish Writing in the Twentieth Century: A Reader*. Cork University Press.
---, (2005) *Light Freedom and Song: A cultural History of Modern Irish Writing*. Yale University Press.
PLATO, *The Republic*. Penguin, 1974.
POLLIO, H., BARLOW, J. AND FINE, H. (1977) *The Poetics of Growth: Figurative Language in Psychology, Psychotherapy, and Education*. NJ: Lawrence Erlbaum.
PRINCETON (THE NEW) ENCYCLOPEDIA OF POETRY AND POETICS (1993) (eds. A. Preminger & T.V.F. Brogan). Princeton Univ Press.
RAINE, C. (1978) "An Enquiry into Two Inches of Ivory," *The Onion Memory*. Oxford UP.
---, (1994) *History: The Home Movie*. Penguin.
REDGROVE, P. (1994) "The Olfactors," *New Writing* 3 (eds. A. Motion & C. Rodd). Minerva.
RICE, D. & SCHOFER, P. (1981) "Tropes and Figures: Symbolization and Figuration," *Semiotica* 35-1/2, 93-124.
RICH, A. (1974) *Poems, Selected and New*. New York: Norton.
---, (1986) *Blood, Bread and Poetry: Selected Prose 1979-1985*. London: Virago Press.
---, (1993) *What is Found There: Notebooks on Poetry and Politics*. Norton.
RICHARDS, I.A. (1926) *Science and Poetry*. London.
RICKS, C. (1984) *The Force of Poetry*. Oxford UP.
RICKS, C. & MICHAELS, L. (eds.) (1990) *The State of the Language*. Faber.
RILKE, R. M. (1904) *New Poems*. Trans. J.B. Leishman. London. (1964)
---, (1925) letter of 13 Nov., *Briefe*, ii (Wiesbaden, 1950), 453.
ROBERTS, P.D. (1986) *How Poetry Works*. Penguin.
RODRÍGUEZ, C. (1971) *Poesía, 1953-1966*. Barcelona: Plaza & Janes.
ROGERS, E.M. (ed.) (1982) *Communication and Development: Critical Perspectives*. Sage.
ROSENTHAL, M. (ed.) (1966) *The William Carlos Williams Reader*. NY.
RUVALCABA, E. (1988) *"Apuntes,"* En Breve: Minimalism in Mexican Poetry 1900-1985 (ed. E. Lamadrid). New Mexico: Tooth of Time.
SALINAS, P. (1975) *Poesías completas*. Barcelona.
SANTORO-BRIENZA, L. (1993*) The Tortoise and the Lyre: Aesthetic Reconstructions*. Dublin: Irish Academic Press.
SAPIR, E. (1949) "The Meaning of Religion," *Culture, Language and Personality*. Berkeley: Univ. of California.
SAUSSURE, F. DE (1966) *Course in General Linguistics*. McGraw-Hill.

SEWALL, R.B. (ed.) (1963) *Emily Dickinson: A Collection of Critical Essays*, Prentice-Hall.
SILVER, P.W. (1968) "New Spanish Poetry: the Rodríguez/Brines Generation." *Books Abroad*, 42, 212.
SIMMONS, J. (1987) *Poems 1956-1986*. Newcastle upon Tyne: Bloodaxe.
SINFIELD, A. (ed.) (1983) *Society and Literature 1945-1970*. London: Methuen.
SIRR, P. "Home and Away Pages," Supplement (p.7) *Irish Times*, 30/11/94.
SKINNER, B. F. (1957) *Verbal Behaviour*. New York: Appleton-Century-Crofts.
SKOVMAND, M. & SHRODER, K. (eds.) (1992) *Media Cultures: Reappraising Transnational Media*. Routledge.
SOLT, M.E. (ed.) (1968) *Concrete Poetry*: A World View. Bloomington, Ind.
SPENDER, S. (1962) *The Making of a Poem*. Norton.
STANFORD, W.B. (1980) *Enemies of Poetry*. Routledge.
STEINMETZ, C.P. (1923) *Four Lectures on Relativity and Space*. Montana: Kessinger Publishing, 2005
SUNDAY TIMES (1994) *1000 Makers of the Twentieth Century*.
SWEENEY, M. (1992) *Cacti*. London: Secker & Warburg.
TAMMI, P. (1991) "Text, subtext, intertext: On applying Taranovsky's analytic method (with examples from Finnish poetry)," *Semiotica* 87-3/4, 315-347.
THE POET'S CHAIR: *John Montague, Nuala Ní Dhomhnaill, Paul Durcan: The First Nine Years of the Ireland Chair of Poetry*. Dublin: The Lilliput Press, 2008.
TILLMAN, L. (1991) *Motion Sickness*. London: Serpent's Tail.
TOCCI, G. (1994) "Perceiving the City; Reflections on Early Modern Age," *Critical Quarterly*, vol. 36, no. 4.
TODD, A.C. & HAYWARD, M. (eds.) (1993) *Twentieth Century Russian Poetry*. Selected by Y.Yevtushenko. London: Fourth Estate.
TOMLINSON, C. (1972) *Written on Water*. Oxford UP.
---, (1986) *Collected Poems*. Oxford UP.
TURNER, B.S. (ed.) (1990) *Theories of Modernity and Postmodernity*. London: Sage Publications.
USTINOV, P. (1991) cited in *A Writer's Notebook* (ed. H. Exley) Watford: Exley Publications.
VALÉRY, P. (1958) *The Art of Poetry*. Trans. D. Folliot. NY.
VATTIMO, G. (1988) *The End of Modernity: Nihilism and Hermeneutics in Post-Modern Culture*. Trans. J. R. Snyder. Cambridge: Polity Press.
VERNON, P.E. (ed.) (1970) *Creativity: Selected Readings*. Penguin.
WALCOTT, D. (1986) *Collected Poems*. Faber.
WALLER, R.J. (1993) *The Bridges of Madison County*. London: Heinemann.
WATERSTONE'S GUIDE TO BOOKS (1988) 2nd ed. London.
WATZLAWICK, P. et al (1974) Change: *Principles of Problem Formation and Problem Resolution*. Norton.
WEISSBORT, D. (1989) *Translating Poetry: The Double Labyrinth*.

London: MacMillan.

WENDERS, W. (dir.) (1987) *Wings of Desire* (a film). France/Germany.

WHITMAN, W. (1855) *Leaves of Grass*. Oxford (1990).

WHITWORTH, J. (1983) *Poor Butterflies*. London: Secker & Warburg.

WHORF, B.L. (1978) *Language, Thought and Reality* (ed. J. Carroll).
MIT: Cambridge, Massachusetts.

WILLIAMS, H. (1988) poem published in the *London Review of Books*,
Vol 10, No 22, December.

WILLIAMS, W.C. (1962) *Pictures from Brueghel and other poems*. NY.

---, (1987) *Collected Poems, 1909-1939*. Carcanet.

WILLS, C. (1991) "Contemporary Irish women poets: The privatisation of myth,"
Diverse Voices: Essays on Twentieths Century Women Writers in English, ed.
H.D. Jump (Hemel Hempstead: Harvester Wheatsheaf).

---, (2002) "No longer islanded," *Times Literary Supplement*, no. 5157, 1 Feb.

WILMER, C. (1995) *Poets Talking: The "Poet of the Month" interviews from
BBC Radio 3*. Carcanet.

WILSON, E. (1993) "Tournier, the Body and the Reader," *French Studies*
Vol XLVII No.I.

WILSON, J. (1986) *Octavio Paz*. Boston: Twane Publishers.

WINNER, E. (1982) *Invented Worlds: The Psychology of the Arts*. Cambridge:
Harvard Univ. Press.

WINOKUR, J. (1989) *Writers on Writing*. London: Headline.

WRIGHT, E. (1986) *The Poetry of Protest under Franco*. London:
Tamesis Books.

YARROW, R. (1985) "The potential of consciousness: Towards a new approach
to states of consciousness in literature," *Journal of European Studies* xv March
Part 1, No. 57.

YEATS, W.B. (1990) *Collected Poems* (ed. A. Martin). London: Arena

INDEX

semiosis: mind born out of, 23;
  semiotic insights into poetry, 2, 23,
  25, 29
senses, poetry should appeal to, 55,
  57, 78–79, 87, 93, 131;
  overdeveloped one sense in urban
  society, 62
Shakespeare, William, 31, 37, 54,
  71, 131; different approaches to
  plays, 37; *Hermione (The Winter's
  Tale)*, 54; in translation by
  Pasternak, 131; one hundredth and
  twenty ninth sonnet, 31; *Romeo
  and Juliet*, 21
Shelley, Percy Bysshe, 41, 102
Silver, P.W., 71
Simmons, James: *Didn't He Ramble*,
  65
Sinfield, Alan, 137
Sirr, Peter, 138, 141
Skinner, Burrhus Frederic, 24
Smith, Ian Crichton: *For Poets
  Writing in English over in Ireland*,
  117
Solt, Mary Ellen, 48–49, 52
Sontag, Susan, 99
sound in poetry, 29, 57
Spanish Civil War, 70
Spender, Stephen, 9, 70; *The Making
  of a Poem*, 9
spiritual demands on poetry, 3
St. Patrick, 10
St. Paul, 58, 66; *Second Epistle to
  the Corinthians*, 66
Stalinism, 72
Stanford, Willian Bedell, 13, 32
stanza, original meaning of, 43
Stein, Gertrude, 116
Steinmetz, Charles P., 124
Strong, Eithne, 116
Structuralists, 139
Sweeney, Matthew, 130
Swir, Anna, 102, 119
symbolism, 3–4, 19

Symons, Arthur, 96
sympathetic coincidence, 121

T

taboo subjects in poetry, 19
Tammi, Pekka, 37
Taranovsky method applied to
  intertextuality, 37
Tchaikovsky, Piotr Ilyich, 15
technology, 2, 48–49, 62, 77–81, 83–
  85, 138; its human cost, 77; lethal
  for a young American couple, 84;
  Majakovskij and Crane on, 83;
  poets responded to, 48; telephones
  and televisions, 78; to cocoon
  oneself from the real world, 83;
  unable to deal holistically with
  people, 79; used for inane
  repetition, 85
Tennyson, Alfred, Lord, 32, 48, 62,
  67; on not being understood, 32
third eye, of the mystic, 79
Thomas, Dylan, 32, 60, 63; *Under
  Milkwood*, 60
Tillman, Lynne, 47
time yourself to read a poem, 66
Titley, Alan, 117
Tocci, Giovanni, 121
Todd, Albert, 73
Tolstoy, Leo, 131
Tomlinson, Charles, 12, 43, 53, 62,
  122; *A Meditation on John
  Constable*, 53; *The Demise of the
  Modern Poet*, 44; *The Way of the
  World*, 12
Tournier, Michel, 97
trains, poems on, 55, 101, 127
Transcendental Meditation, 8
translation: a "global satellite", 119;
  a bridge between cultures, 119;
  brings the universal vision closer,
  110; from Gaelic as an act of self-
  understanding, 104; Kinsella tries
  to recapture what was lost in

DATE DUE

Demco, Inc. 38-293